When we think of all the things that need forgiving, we begin to appreciate how vital the spirit of forgiveness is to keep each of us, and all of us together, intact. Forgiveness is not just a thing nice people do. It's not a tactic we might consider for personal improvement or to tidy up our spiritual lives. As the world we live in spirals toward greater feats of injustice, greed, violence, and bigotry, the reasons to forgive mount astronomically. The cost of unforgiveness, too, becomes ever more apparent. Forgiveness reveals itself to be not just one possible option for the future but the only viable chance we've got to have a future.

The human race must learn to forgive, to practice forgiveness, to choose it, to seek it, to value it, and to want it. That means each of us individually must do the same, because the world begins in the human heart.

THE FORGIVENESS BOOK

A Catholic Approach

Alice Camille & Paul Boudreau

acta
PUBLICATIONS

THE FORGIVENESS BOOK
A Catholic Approach
by Alice Camille and Paul Boudreau

Edited by Gregory F. Augustine Pierce
Cover by Tom A. Wright
Text design and typesetting by Patricia A. Lynch

Published by ACTA Publications, 5559 W. Howard Street, Skokie, IL 60077-2621, (800) 397-2282, www.actapublications.com

Library of Congress Catalog number: 2008925898

ISBN: 978-0-87946-356-4

Printed in the United States of America by Versa Press

Year 15 14 13 12 11 10 09 08

Printing 15 14 13 12 11 10 9 8 7 6 5 4 3 2 First

♻ Cover printed on Rainbow 17 from Ecological Fibers, Inc.
Text printed n 30% post-consumer waste paper

CONTENTS

In gratitude to our friend Erin J. Boulton,
who has learned well
all the hard lessons about forgiveness
and has shown us how it's done.

This Business of Forgiveness

Nobody ever forgets where he buried a hatchet.
— Kin Hubbard, American humorist

Most of us are not crazy about the forgiveness business. Why forgive? When we get mad at someone, after all, we've got reasons for it. That person has "trespassed against us," as the saying goes—literally, he or she has crossed a line that shouldn't be crossed. That leaves us hurt, offended, or tried beyond the breaking point of our patience. If we should entertain that anger for more than a day, it's likely to go into cold storage for a season or longer, in the interior vault marked "resentment." There the original outrage and our response to it becomes part of us, a possession as real and solid as any treasure.

When it comes to storing offenses however, such "treasure" is not valued or welcome. Emotionally speaking, it's radioactive, the sort of thing that requires a special team in hazmat suits to go in and extract. But where will that special team come from to relieve us of the hazardous material of our resentment? Who can bring relief and healing, and restore wholeness to our relationships?

The work of forgiveness may seem like an ugly job, but somebody's got to do it. Truth is, the alternative to forgiveness is far uglier: hardened hearts, broken relationships, memories full of shrapnel, and families or communities paralyzed and divided. The territory of unforgiveness is also perilous, fraught with insecurity and danger: just ask citizens of Northern Ireland, the Middle East, Africa, or the fractured neighborhoods of any modern city close to home. The interior landscape of unforgiveness in the human heart is just as unlivable as the one outside. If there's a way out of this personal horror of resentment and hatred, many people would love to find it.

Forgiveness is the way, and it is possible. But it isn't, strictly speaking, natural; that is, it isn't according to our nature. Forgiveness has to be chosen, and we have to choose it, or the healing won't begin. This is the flipside of free will that we don't always consider. Being free to do what we want means living with the consequences of what we choose. We need to make thoughtful choices to avoid the pre-set defaults of human nature, and a soured, bitter, vindictive heart is the default result of a life lived without deliberate acts of forgiveness.

Recently the two of us writing this book attended a workshop on forgiveness at a parish in a nearby town. Unfamiliar with

> ✦ Forgiveness has to be chosen, and we have to choose it, or the healing won't begin.

the church grounds, we wandered around for a while looking for an open door. Finally, we spotted a priest hurrying by with his arms full of materials. "Is this the way to the workshop?" one of us called out.

"Forgiveness? Over there," the priest replied, directing us to the adjacent parish hall. And then mischievously he added, "And condemnation? Over there!" pointing back to the church. We all laughed ruefully, acknowledging that sometimes we do experience our relationship to the church as a likely encounter with disapproval.

What's even more rueful is that, even when the divergent paths of forgiveness and condemnation are clearly pointed out to us, all too often we go down the path of condemnation anyway. Why would we do that? Perhaps it's because condemnation is the more familiar route. Have you ever taken a wrong turn on a strange road, only to repeat the error each time you come to that same spot? Once reinforced, a pattern establishes itself and gets harder to break the longer we pursue it. If condemnation is the way we habitually go—if it's the rule under which we were raised and is repeated in subsequent relationships—it will be that much more difficult to take a fresh route to a forgiving future.

If forgiveness is so unnatural, unpracticed, and hard to do, then why should we forgive? The best reason is because it is the only road to freedom. Every other way—condemnation, blaming, open hostility, self-righteousness, hidden resentment, cold anger, cynicism, frozen emotions, pretense—entraps us in the pain that originally caused the breech of relationship. Without forgiveness, we can only multiply enemies and isolation. In time, those who cannot forgive will find the avenue of love less available as the boulevard of self-defense and self-justification grows ever wider.

Our world is full of heartache, much of it unavoidable. But the special brand of anguish that comes from the unwillingness to forgive is something we don't have to live with. Whether you are seeking forgiveness for yourself or hope to find the capacity to forgive someone else, it's time to forge a new way.

This book is subtitled *A Catholic Approach*. We did so for two reasons. One is that we both come from the Roman Catholic tradition. We are a religious educator and a pastor.

This approach is also "catholic" in the sense that it is universally applicable. Catholics don't have a lock on the forgiveness process. Forgiveness is an ideal shared by all religious traditions and people of good will. Because the authors are pastoral ministers, we've seen the damage that unforgiveness causes in marriages, families, and whole communities, not to mention what it does to the individuals who struggle with the pain of unhealed past injuries. We're convinced that forgiveness is the only sure route to healing, and the only way for followers of Jesus to put their faith into practice. No one can believe in the God of mercy and deny that same mercy to others. People can't receive the free and full amnesty of grace for their own sinfulness and still demand that those around them pay for their offenses.

We may not be experts in forgiveness, but we are among the grateful recipients of God's generous gift of it. Out of trust in God's mercy, in the hope of our own healing, for the love of Jesus, we dare to offer some words about the wonder of forgiveness and how it is ultimately the last best lifestyle for this world...and the next.

May the peace of Christ heal and claim your heart!

Alice Camille
Paul Boudreau

No One Said It Would Be Easy

I would not be surprised if hostility, anger, resentment and hatred proved to be the greatest stumbling blocks to our spiritual growth. — Henri J. M. Nouwen

"I don't want to see a chaplain!" the woman in the bed screamed. It was Claire's first night as a hospital chaplain-in-training, and this was only her second visit to a sick room. All she had to guide her on her rounds was a piece of paper with the names and room numbers of people who had checked her religious affiliation on the hospital admission forms. The young woman had slipped into this darkened ward after receiving a mumbled response to her knock. But the woman in the bed was outraged by Claire's presence before the young chaplain had a chance to do more than introduce herself.

As Claire backed out of the room apologetically, the woman continued shouting across the space between them. "Don't bring God in here! God's the one who let this happen to me! Why didn't that drunk who hit me with his car wind up here instead of me? Why am I the one who's going to pay for *his* mistake for the *rest of my life*?" Claire stopped at the door, listening.

> ❀ Forgiveness may be the solution, but first we must—honestly and without flinching—address and honor the underlying problems that lead to hurt.

If the woman was going to keep talking, the least she could do, as God's representative, was to pay attention.

So the woman screamed out her rage, pain, and despair for a long time. Her body was broken, her sense of justice violated, her fear for the future immense, and her faith in the God of love and simple decency deeply challenged. Into the chasm of such genuine anguish, what could Claire possibly add that would not be hopelessly inadequate? The woman's suffering was so hugely present that to talk of healing, compassion, or forgiveness would be like putting up pious wallpaper in a house that was on fire.

Healing, compassion, and forgiveness were vital to this woman's well-being, Claire was sure. But she was also certain that the time for speaking a living word had not yet arrived. For now, listening was better.

Although forgiveness is very possibly the final answer to every form of violence encountered in our world, it cannot be the first response in every situation. Forgiveness may be the solution, but first we must—honestly and without flinching—address and honor the underlying problems that lead to hurt and anger in the first place.

What we have done and failed to do

Human offenses come in all sizes: overwhelming enough to dev-
astate a nation, or incisive enough to cut a single heart in two.
We have only to think of the legacy of apartheid in South Africa,
the wars of the last century (some of which are still ongoing), or
the ongoing nightmare of terrorism around the globe to know
how far hatred can compel humanity into acts of utter inhu-
manity. Under certain circumstances, many of us seem willing
to cancel our obligations toward other groups of people to the
point of erasing their claim to personhood altogether. How, we
must wonder, does the Palestinian forgive the Jew, the Jew the
Nazi, the black man the white one, the poor woman the rich
one, or the victim the criminal?

We can't address the big picture of human division without first considering its hidden roots: the fear, shame, prejudice,
past injury or present injustice that create the interior environment in which such outrages occur. How do the social systems
around us support discrimination, inequality, and prejudice?
How may structures we count on—such as schools, organized
religions, businesses, news media, and government—wittingly
or unwittingly assist in forming climates of suspicion, antagonism, and ongoing division?

Even nearer to us is the web of family relationships that contributes its own share of unreconciled burdens. What injustice
or abuse did we receive from grandparents or parents, living or
deceased, that still afflicts us today? What have we suffered in
marriage or in a significant love relationship that contributes to
bitterness and loss of self-esteem? How may our children have
caused pain by abandoning our values or ignoring our advice?
Have friends betrayed us, sisters or brothers turned their backs
on us, or important mentors abandoned us at a critical time?

Those blessed with picture-perfect families and intimate relationships may still suffer violation from an unexpected source:
criminal attack, sudden illness, disabling accident, and "acts of
God" such as tornado, earthquake, flood, or fire. Those whom
we love may be lost to us by circumstances outside our control,
most poignantly to suffering and death.

Under the influence of these burdens, both social and personal, our hearts may encounter a tug-of-war that threatens to
extinguish our capacity for love, trust, and peace. The need to
forgive so many wrongs in the world "as is" often reaches into
the most private sanctuary of all: the relationship between us
and our God. Considering how many reasons we have to em-
ploy forgiveness over the course of a lifetime, the real wonder is
that the task isn't given more attention in our personal forma-
tion. Rarely are we taught lessons of forgiveness in school, or
shown models of it in our upbringing. It is not proclaimed often
enough in our pulpits or held up in civic affairs as a working
aspect of domestic or foreign policy. If anything, forgiveness is
often viewed in matters public and private as a weakness, a mar-
ginal route only sissies, wimps, and flower children might take.
Real grownups, we are taught, don't forgive. They wipe out the
enemy, superhero-style!

Forgiveness has become the road not taken in addressing human conflicts. A friend of ours relates the experience of growing
up as a "bully magnet." Being small, skinny, redheaded, and much
freckled, his problem was compounded by a gentle nature and a
bad stutter. One day, after being pummeled by the usual culprit,
our friend decided to try a new approach. Regaining his foot-
ing, he extended a hand to his persecutor. "You won; it was a fair
fight," he offered. "So now let's be friends." The bully, confounded
by this unanticipated turn of events, beat him up again.

Before forgiveness can become part of the normal arsenal of responses, accepted as a reasonable alternative to bearing a grudge or seeking revenge, it may need to be popularly rehabilitated as an honorable choice, even a noble one, in the stories of our culture. The way of forgiveness may also need to be taught in workshops both secular and spiritual, so that the skills and self-understanding necessary to begin the process may be available to all of us.

Honesty as a starting point

"You take the high road and I'll take the low road," an old song begins. When it comes to responding to offense and injury, few would disagree that the way of forgiveness is one of the high roads available to us. But the high road is rarely the easiest route, so it's not surprising that many of us gravitate toward the low road. We surrender to the impulse to write off the offender temporarily or permanently from our acquaintance. Or we maintain an outwardly polite relationship but close the door to further trust and intimacy. We may insist on formal apologies, changes in behavior, or restitution for losses before we can even consider forgiving someone. In some cases, there may simply be no conditions under which our friendship or affection can be restored.

Much of the time, our pain, anger, or sadness has real justification. It's grounded in an injury that cannot be dismissed as insignificant. Even when our emotional response may be misplaced or exaggerated, it is not possible for us to swallow it, grin and bear it, or ignore it. Feelings are what they are: indicators of the most primary and primitive experience of being. They color our ability to reason through the complexities of loyalty, connection, and truth, among other issues. We may hold strong

religious convictions that we should love our enemies and forgive those who trespass against us. Yet we still find ourselves at
a loss to actually do those things when the time comes.

Instinctively, we know this much: It isn't enough to give lip
service to phrases of forgiveness when our hearts aren't in it.
How much is it worth to hear someone say "I'm sorry," when we
know he or she isn't? What good is
an apology when experience tells us
another round of the same offensive
behavior is just around the corner?
Obviously, authentic forgiveness can
only be achieved when contrition is
more than words and goes deeper
than mere regret. When we give or
receive forgiveness, we want to see a substantial change in the
very nature of the relationship. If there is no evidence of that
evolution, forgiveness is just a game that none of us really cares
to play.

> ❧ How finished is our
> "closure" on circumstances
> that remain unreconciled
> and unforgiven?

Because the pain and anger caused by offense is so unpleasant to carry around, cutting off the relationship altogether often
seems the only way to "dump" the emotional burden. The fact
that ending a relationship seldom releases us from the difficult
feelings does not seem to deter us from repeating this attempt
at a solution over and over. Just recall a job you quit in disgust,
a former boss you detested, an old romantic attachment that
ended badly, a childhood betrayal you suffered. Do the old feelings arise like incense the moment you reopen the memory?
How finished is our "closure" on circumstances that remain unreconciled and unforgiven?

So far, it seems clear that forgiveness can't be had at the touch
of a button. Nor can we simply jettison the situation of offense

along with the offender and rid ourselves of the trouble. A third way involves the path of honest exploration of what happened and how we really feel about it. This means getting past powerful secondary reactions to the originating ones, which are not always what we think they are. Although we are most immediately aware of being mad at someone after a perceived offense, anger is often a defensive response covering a primary experience of hurt, fear, shame, insecurity, or embarrassment. Writing down the story may help uncover our root emotions about the experience. Talking it out with an objective listener—a counselor, spiritual director, or impartial friend—may also be useful.

Acknowledging the nature of the offense and our real feelings about it is crucial to the business of forgiveness, because papering over these elements with fake indifference ("Who cares?") or polite pretense ("It's okay, I forgive you") will not advance the cause of authentic forgiveness at all. What happened in the past is a reality that cannot be changed. How we feel about it is a factor that should not be dismissed. What happens next, however, is a decision that has yet to be made.

Anger can help

Anger may not be the primary reaction to an offense, but it is frequently a secondary and very prominent player. Too bad that anger has a very bad reputation. It made the fatal "cut" on the exclusive list of Seven Deadly Sins, for one thing. And many of us have suffered the effects of someone else's anger often enough to know that it is an undesirable experience, on either side of the equation. At times anger can become a destructive force, crashing through boundaries and damaging relationships to the point of causing physical harm. The fact that anger can be used in violent ways, however, does not make the substance of anger necessarily destructive. It has its positive side, as Dr. Joan Muller points out in her book, *Is Forgiveness Possible?*:

> Anger defends the self from further or continued abuse, creates needed distance and boundaries, and can provide the energy needed to come to creative and constructive solutions.

Victims of abusive situations such as domestic violence or unfair work practices need to harness their anger before they find the will to act against the powers that are threatening their well-being. Anger is a highly motivating and focusing personal resource. It is the signal that there is some place we need to get to and it provides the energy to get there. But where?

The monks who compiled the list of so-called "deadly" sins centuries ago were trying to give us a map for the journey when they named this list, properly, the capital offenses. The word comes from the Latin for *caput*, "head." The capital sins weren't really sins at all, but rather dispositions at the trailhead of human discernment. When we experience one of these urgent motivations—anger, pride, greed, jealousy, lust, gluttony, or sloth—we have the opportunity to consider what to do with the compelling forces arising within us. Sure, we can clench our fists, steal the watch, engage the gossip, or flop on the sofa when those impulses arise. But here at the trailhead, we can also choose to take the high road away from temptation instead of descending into the darker side of our natures.

Recognizing the signal that anger provides—that movement is required—will help us harness the energy it supplies to make constructive choices. Are there hidden truths that must be spoken out loud? Are there decisions to be made, changes to consider, alternatives that haven't been tried? Something in the present circumstance is clearly unacceptable, and anger comes to defend our interests even when we may be reluctant to do it ourselves. Without screaming our lungs out or swinging our fists, such anger can be purposefully expressed. When we come to the trailhead of anger, it is not necessary to make a descent into darkness.

Psychology teaches that anger presents us with three possibilities: denial, expression, and forgiveness. Denial is the choice to slam the door on an emotion that surprises or dismays us. If we chronically choose to deny anger, it's usually because we were taught to do so by angry or anger-suppressing parents. Denial doesn't eliminate anger, but only sweeps it under the carpet "for now." In fact, regular repression of anger can lead to depression, an inversion of the mountain of energy that is routinely forced underground. Over the long haul, repressed anger can lead to a host of physical and mental disorders.

The second possibility that anger presents—its expression— can be positive and helpful under the right circumstances, as we have indicated. But negative expressions of anger are more common. Chronically uncontrolled anger can produce free-floating aggression that gets assigned to any and all relationships. Conflict then becomes our essential means of relating to others. Dr. Muller points out that destruction fantasies—blowing up the office, shooting the neighbor's dog, pounding away at a cranky child, or even suicidal thoughts—become part of the interior framework of a person who indulges habitual anger. Such a person will also experience rage increasingly disproportionate to each ensuing offense. If we routinely justify our anger without examining it, we may be masking a sea of unresolved needs as potentially destructive of others as they are to ourselves.

Perhaps the most dangerous element of anger lies in its

power to compel us to focus on *it* and not on the person in trouble—namely, ourselves. As professor Dr. John Patton has noted in his work on forgiveness, it is not the rage but "the *heart* or self *with the rage in it* that is the problem." If we address that heart or self, we can abate the anger.

The final choice available to us at the trailhead of anger, then, is forgiveness. But how in the world do we get there from here?

What is forgiveness?

Deep down, we know what forgiveness is or what it ought to be. But since we've all been recipients of "forgiveness talk" in situations that were no more than emotional blackmail or religious pretense, it would be helpful to establish a healthy definition of forgiveness for the purposes of this conversation. It might be best to start by exploring what forgiveness isn't, to eliminate the phantoms from the beginning:

❧ **Forgiveness is not ignoring an offense.** On the contrary, it's recognizing that an offense has occurred, which I must acknowledge, experience with full awareness of my reactions, and for which I must formulate a response.

❧ **Forgiveness is not forgetting.** My brain is hardwired to remember, which enables me to learn. Forgiveness means constantly affirming my intention and resolution to love beyond the offense each time I recollect it. Forgiveness is not a single act of the will done once and completely. It happens on deeper levels each time. As Trappist Father William Menninger says, don't waste your woundedness—make use of it!

❧ **Forgiveness does not mean "it's all right."** Forgiveness will not change the objective facts in a conflict. Wrongdoing certainly is not all right. I am not condoning anything by offering forgiveness. Even though someone has done wrong to me, I can decide to forego retaliatory behavior, punishment, and revenge, preferring to be reconciled.

❧ **Forgiveness doesn't absolve the offender.** Absolution is God's to bestow. I am not assuming that kind of importance in a person's life, nor should I imagine myself in a morally superior position. Forgiveness is good for the forgiver as well as the forgiven. Both of us need the exchange to take place. But I'm not responsible for the response of the other. I'm only responsible for the action I take.

❧ **Forgiveness is not a form of self-sacrifice.** Forgiveness is something I need for my own wholeness. There is simply no room in my heart for all the resentment I would have to carry if I failed to forgive. Nor can bitterness co-exist with all the love I hope to share. Something's got to go. Far from being an act of self-sacrifice, forgiveness is a form of self-interest.

On the positive side, here are some of the affirmations we can make about the task of forgiving:

❧ **Forgiveness is letting somebody off the hook.** When I forgive someone, I release that person from "vexatious obligation": the annoying and distressful energy of a relationship in which offense has taken a commanding role. I set the person free.

❧ **Forgiveness is participation in the benign energy of the universe.** This energy always creates new life and moves toward goodness. Christians commonly call that uncreated energy God, whose likeness we bear. Forgiveness involves turning away from the desire to do harm, regardless of the justification. Forgiveness, in this sense, sets me free, whether or not the other person asks for it or even wants it.

Forgiveness is an invitation to wholeness. When violent words, actions, or emotions erupt in my life, people can be quickly reduced to objects of my wrath. Likewise, I can become entirely focused on and identified with my injury. The choice to forgive invites my adversary, and me, back into personhood.

Forgiveness is at the same time a "work" and a "grace." It is something I do and something God does. My initiation of the process by an act of will is crucial—God will not trespass on my freedom to choose unforgiveness. But I don't have to do "forgiveness" all by myself, nor can I expect to.

Conclusion

We began this chapter with a real story of a young chaplain dealing with a deeply injured woman. In this case, the woman's wounds were obviously physical—but they also went far deeper, interlaced with emotional and spiritual anguish that caused her undeniable suffering. An accident at the hands of a drunk driver compelled her to fiercely accuse the man who had crippled her. But in her own words the woman also gave voice to the dreadful penetration of the violence she had experienced: It had severed her confidence in God and robbed her of the possibility of hope. Before all else, her road to healing would have to begin with forgiving God. It should not surprise us that the road to forgiveness often emerges at God's doorstep.

How Can I Lay This Burden Down?

Unless souls are saved, nothing is saved;
there can be no world peace unless there is soul peace...
for nothing happens in the external world that has not first
happened within a soul. — *Archbishop Fulton J. Sheen*

Mrs. Audet was not going to the wedding and that was final. Her daughter Nicole was getting married in a month, but the mother of the bride wouldn't be there. You see, this was Nicole's second marriage and it was being performed in a Congregational Church. Nicole's first husband had been a cruel man who abused her physically for years. When he began abusing the children, however, that was all Nicole was going to take and she divorced him. But Mrs. Audet was a devout Catholic and her daughter's first marriage was in a Catholic church. The mother knew the second marriage wasn't the real deal in the eyes of the Church, so she was boycotting the wedding. She believed that's what a good Catholic should do. After all, she didn't want to lend credence to Nicole's departure from the Catholic Church in which she had been brought up.

But there were serious reasons for the failure of Nicole's first marriage. It was a sordid tale of broken promises, infidelities, and abuse. "But I told her," Mrs. Audet would say whenever she recounted the story, "that divorce is a sin. Marriage is for life and she had to stick it out." Then she would add: "Just like I did."

The truth is that Mrs. Audet was caught up in a complex web of resentment, bitterness, and a heartfelt but misinformed devotion to her religion that seriously threatened to sabotage her relationship with her daughter. Mrs. Audet had suffered through a painful, forty-year marriage, filled with cruelty until her husband's death, believing it was the right thing to do. Her daughter Nicole, growing up in that household and learning about marriage from the only model of marriage she had, had unconsciously sought a similar relationship with her own first spouse. When Nicole later told her mother of her husband's abuse, Mrs. Audet made it clear to Nicole that divorce was not an option and she should learn to endure the situation. Nicole hung in there for a while, but when it became too dangerous for her and her children, she finally got a divorce. Now she was going to marry a much different kind of man, but because she would not or could not get an annulment from the Catholic Church, she was getting married in her new husband's Protestant church.

Nicole's divorce and later plans to remarry mounted a serious challenge to Mrs. Audet's understanding of the way things were supposed to be. She remained terribly bitter about her own unhappy marriage and, at some level, resented her daughter's choice to do what she herself had wanted to do but felt unable to reach for because of her religious convictions. Mrs. Audet didn't know it, but refusing to attend Nicole's wedding was a form of punishment she was inflicting on her daughter for pursuing the happiness that she herself had never been able to attain.

The mother needed to acknowledge the intensity of her anger toward the circumstances of her own marriage and the hidden resentment she felt about her daughter escaping from the same nightmare. She also needed to hear that, according to correct Catholic teaching, Nicole had both the right and the responsibility to abandon her abusive situation in order to protect herself and her children and seek happiness, even if it meant getting a divorce and being remarried outside the Catholic church. The understanding Mrs. Audet had of her religion and the early guidance she was given concerning her marriage reflected an interpretation of the rules that was hopelessly legalistic, lacked in any pastoral sensibility, and failed to recognize and serve the dignity of her own life. Under the circumstances, Mrs. Audet had a lot of forgiving to do. She needed to forgive her own husband for the cruelty he had inflicted on her. And she needed to forgive herself for putting up with it. Also, she needed to forgive God and the Catholic Church. The one she did not have to forgive was her daughter.

Why is it so hard to forgive?

The most common problem we have laying down the burdens of resentment and bitterness is not that we don't want to forgive but that it just seems impossible. Or else we simply don't know how to begin.

Let's look at some of the contributing factors to the problem, starting with a simple metaphor about cars. The economy of auto repair always seeks to find the simplest explanation for what goes wrong. If the car won't run, the first thing a good mechanic does is check to see if there is gas in the tank. If there's no fuel, the car doesn't go anywhere. Problem solved.

✻ **Forgiveness is dynamic, a kind of living energy. It's not just something that we offer; it must be obtained as well.**

The same is true for forgiveness. When we have trouble forgiving, the first thing we need to do is look in our forgiveness tank. If it's empty, we've found the problem. Forgiveness is dynamic, a kind of living energy. It's not just something that we offer; it must be obtained as well. We can't give it to others unless it is first given to us. And the primary "gas station" of forgiveness—the place where we learn the customs and traditions of mercy and are taught how to forgive—is the home in which we grew up and the faith community in which we were raised.

Unfortunately, not all children are raised in an environment where forgiveness is readily practiced. We learn early that there are things we do that will get us into trouble. Parents inflict punishment on children for their wrongdoing—some more, some less—but most at least a little. Fear of penalty is thought by most parents to be a great deterrent, but more often it motivates the offender to be more cautious and discreet, and to discover artful ways of not getting caught. This behavior nurtures a kind of double life in which we present a good and well-behaved appearance, while at the same time maintaining a hidden life of petty little wicked deeds that would, if discovered, invite disapproval and even punishment from the world around us.

This dark side of our lives expands as we grow older and

find more serious things to do wrong. At the same time, we may gain a little knowledge about religion—and we know how dangerous a *little* knowledge can be. We discover that there's a source of cosmic condemnation and punishment higher than our parents: an all-seeing God from whom we cannot hide our skullduggery, a divine Judge who will, eventually, bring justice to bear against all we have done. That's when things start getting complicated. We might be able to dodge our parents' reprisals; but how are we to escape God's?

What seems worse is that religion tends to expand our understanding of the wrong that we do. It was bad enough trying to get past our parents' laws with life and limb intact. Now we find out that God has rules too, which carry an *eternal* penalty if they are broken. We also learn that *thoughts* can get us in as much trouble as words and deeds. Additionally, our religious tradition may have its own set of regulations. Running afoul of the technicalities of worship and religious practice can carry equally onerous and endless consequences. It's a real pickle.

All told, by the time we grow up, the mechanism of guilt has bound us pretty well to the reward/punishment system. Our parents, knowingly or unknowingly and to greater or lesser extent, have used guilt to control our behavior. And we're not talking about bad parents here. We're talking about *good* parents who use reward and punishment for our benefit, to make us better people. Still, it leaves us with a big knot of fear tied around our lives, a kind of moral cage in which judgment and condemnation are the door and the lock. And the church, unfortunately, instead of being the "school of forgiveness" it's supposed to be, can raise the reward/punishment paradigm to an absolute, other-worldly level. Instead of being grounded for a week, you're grounded *forever*.

Behind the door

Locked inside the reward/punishment system, we are compelled to live according to it. Therefore when we think or say
or do something against the moral code—the laws of parents,
God, or religion—the system generates guilt and we feel bad
about it. Now, that's not necessarily a problem. Guilt can keep
us on a fairly decent path. It motivates us to feed the kids, take
care of Grandma, and mow the lawn.

But our own sense of guilt also energizes our impulse to
judge others, and therein lies the difficulty. Just as when we
cause offense we experience judgment and condemnation, so
too when people offend us we seek judgment and condemnation
against them. As long as we're locked in the reward/punishment
system, we *participate* in the system. The powerful upwelling of
outrage and indignation we feel when offended is the product
of growing up in an environment where our own offensive behavior provoked outrage and indignation from those around us.
And just as we were punished by those whom we offended, we
in turn feel compelled to punish those who offend us.

It's not hard to draw the connection between our experiences growing up and the behavior we exhibit when faced with
offenses. Walking out on someone or refusing to talk to that person has its roots in being put in the corner or sent to our rooms.
The isolation imposed on us for our wrongdoing becomes the
isolation we impose on others. The shouting and arguing we
participate in as adults comes from the shouting and arguing we
were subjected to in childhood. In extreme cases, the violence
and abuse we received as children becomes the violence and
abuse we dish out as grownups.

Opening the door

So, why can't we just "forgive and forget?" First of all, forgetting is not possible. We're designed to remember, especially those events that generate great emotion. The memory of some truly awful thing that happens to us may sometimes be repressed, but it is never forgotten.

Forgiveness is never a matter of forgetting. As American psychiatrist Thomas Szasz wrote, "The stupid neither forgive nor forget; the naïve forgive and forget; the wise forgive but do not forget." But in order to be able to forgive, we must first be forgiven.

Forgiveness is the treasure of the gospels, the pearl of great price. It shows up unexpectedly in our lives; we stumble upon it without warning. It is first discovered, then pondered in amazement, then possessed, and finally savored and shared for a lifetime. Forgiveness is the key that sets us free and, at the same time, draws us on a lifelong quest to its source, which is love. It's the gift of God that makes hope possible, gives joy beyond the moment, and sustains faith for a lifetime. When we finally find out that forgiveness is ours and gather it in, we will at last be at peace with God, parents, old adversaries, new relationships, and the world around us. And once the forgiveness tank is filled to the top and running over, sharing that forgiveness with others becomes possible.

The movement from living in fear to living out forgiveness is called "conversion." It is when we are **fully** forgiven that we can forgive. The power of forgiveness is infinite and eternal. Because it is a living energy, it flows *through* **us,** carrying away our offenses and moving out from us to forgive the offenses of others. When we are forgiven, we are truly free and become able to forgive others so they can be free as well.

The issue of justice

"An eye for an eye," the Bible says, "and a tooth for a tooth." Sometimes people use this ancient dictum as a kind of launching platform for the pursuit of what is widely considered to be justice. After all, what's fair is fair and people should get what's coming to them. If you've been offended by people, it seems that you have the right to offend them back.

The most primitive form of justice is what we see operating in the everyday events of life. It is the cause-and-effect relationship between actions and their consequences. For instance, if someone steps off the curb to cross a busy street without first carefully looking both ways for oncoming traffic, that person may experience a version of swift justice for the mistake. If he got run over by a bus, we could say, it would be his own fault. He experienced the natural consequences of his own ill-advised actions—assuming he was healthy, clear-headed, and possessed a minimal understanding of how one goes about crossing a street.

Members of society may hold to a similar system of justice. The rules of society establish standards of behavior to which the members must adhere or face the consequences. The penalty for breaking these laws can be the payment of a fine, removal from the society and incarceration, rescinding of privileges, and even physical punishment. "Ignorance of the law is no excuse," the judge will tell you. The bus will hit you even if you don't see it coming. So worldly justice demands that offenders pay the price.

The principles of this kind of justice—we can call it "retributive" or "punitive" justice—are frequently carried over into our personal relationships. We'll tend to push back if we are pushed. If something of ours is taken, we'll certainly demand it back. If we're injured in some way, we'll insist that the guilty party be held responsible. If people break the rules, they must pay the penalty. It's only natural.

But there is a better way. We believe that the Great Creative Power of the universe, a just and exacting judge, accomplishes the finest and final justice of all through forgiveness and healing. We Catholics call this justice "restorative."

Using the example of the fellow stepping out in front of the bus, we see the primary justice of creation kicking in when the poor guy gets run over. One of two things will happen next: he will live or he will die. If he lives, all the energy in creation will work together to bring about healing. His body will mend completely or partially and he will adapt to his new situation. In all likelihood, he will amend his ways and cross streets with more care in the future.

> ✿ Forgiveness has this power: to reclaim what was lost and to bring a person to a better place—the fulfillment of every good possibility.

If he dies, in faith we believe his life will continue. The consequence of his "choice," however blindly made, is death; but faith tells us that he does not drop into a void of nothingness from which he will never emerge. We believe eternal life means just that: beyond the mystery of death, existence has no beginning and no end. So when the bus renders his body no longer able to sustain life—the moment we call death—we believe a rescue is effected and the man survives, albeit on the other side of the mystery.

In both cases, while on the primitive level of justice the fellow "pays for his sin," on a higher level the sublime goodness of restorative justice seeks to renew that which has been corrupted by the wrong choice and reestablish the goodness and peace that was present before the choice was made. Forgiveness has this power: to reclaim what was lost and to bring a person to a better place—the fulfillment of every good possibility.

Why should we forgive?

It's always tiring to bear a burden, whether the load is bricks or bitterness, rocks or resentment. Hoisting it and carrying it around wherever we go weighs us down, saps our energy, hurts our bodies, and leaves us weary.

What kind of human energy do we generate when we hold a grudge? Fundamentally, it makes us feel bad. Anyone who's ever suffered a bout of rage knows the kind of physical experiences such emotions stir up. The chemistry in our bodies causes us to tremble and shake, and can even make us sick.

Justin will tell you all about it. He was driving into the next town to pick up some parts he needed for a job back at the shop. Midday traffic was light and he was in the fast lane, cruising at his usual "plus-ten," the 10-mile-per-hour margin over the speed limit that the police customarily allowed on this stretch of freeway. He was quickly overtaking another car in his lane moping along at a pokey "minus-five," so he flashed his head-lights, signaling the other driver to move right to a slower lane. The other driver didn't budge. This thoughtless driving behavior annoyed Justin to no end. By law, slower traffic was supposed to move to the right to allow faster cars—even cars going over the speed limit—to safely pass. But this guy was hogging the fast lane and wasn't moving out of the way.

So Justin crept up on the other guy's bumper and flashed his lights again. Still the driver wouldn't move. Justin was really getting angry now. He wasn't in a hurry; it was the principle of the thing. The law was on his side; the other driver was supposed to move out of the way. Justin inched closer still, flashing his lights again and again. But the other guy didn't budge. Now Justin was livid. He swerved to the right into the next lane and pulled up alongside the other car. He gestured rudely to the other driver, using the universal sign of disapproval. Then he pulled ahead and in retaliation swung abruptly back into the fast lane, missing the other guy's front bumper by inches.

Justin wasn't finished. In a final gesture of his annoyance, he slowed suddenly, forcing the other guy to hit his brakes. Then satisfied, Justin pulled away.

It was after he had settled back down to his normal speed that Justin noticed his hands were shaking. In fact, he was trembling all over, his heart was beating fast, and he felt a kind of roiling deep in his stomach. His mouth was dry and he was breathing like he had just run up the stairs. It was then that it occurred to him: He had just had a bout of what they call "road rage." He could feel the effects of it, and it wasn't very pleasant.

Justin's body was reacting to the event he had just experienced. The conflict, the anger, and the danger of his encounter with the other driver had produced in him the "fight or flight" response. This is the human body's primitive biological reaction to a perceived threat and the need to put up a defense (fight) or make an escape (flight). It results when large amounts of adrenaline are released into the bloodstream to prepare the human body for extreme physical action. It accelerates heart and lung, inhibits digestion and constricts blood vessels in many parts of the body, raises blood pressure, and releases nutrients into the system to provide energy for intense muscular effort.

The fight or flight response worked really well in prehistoric times, when primitive cave-dwellers had to fight for their very existence or run from hungry saber-toothed tigers in order to avoid becoming lunch. But modern western society poses few such threats, so the chemistry of this extreme survival reaction can become destructive to the human body. Many disorders, such as ulcers, high blood pressure, and heart disease, are linked to the effects of stress on the body.

The way of peace

An athlete can put this fight/flight chemistry to work. A football player can use the fuel being pumped into his muscles to overcome his counterpart on the other team. A boxer can hit harder or take a harder punch. A tennis player can chase down wide shot, or a baseball player can remain ready and alert to run after a fly ball. But what can a driver behind the wheel do? Or a spouse across the dinner table? Or parents watching television with the kids in the living room? What can any of us do with this potent physiological cocktail when we perceive that our peace, our values, or our well-being has been threatened by another?

What Justin could have done was simply move to the right and drive by the other guy, a maneuver that is generally allowed by law when the other person fails to yield the lane. Or, if that were not possible, he could have waited patiently until a lane was clear and he had a chance to pass. But for such a controlled response to be possible, Justin would have to change the way he looked at others and what he believed to be his own role at the center of the universe.

For instance, Justin could consider that not all slow drivers hogging the fast lane are doing so out of ill intent. Suppose some were dyslexic and actually thought they were in the slow lane? It's possible. The other driver could just be ignorant of the rules. And even if the other guy was a thoughtless jerk, how could Justin tell that was the case without knowing the man personally? What it comes down to is that, for whatever reason, Justin's best move would be to let the guy off the hook and go on his way. "If someone takes what is rightfully yours," Jesus teaches in the gospel, "don't demand it back."

We can and need to apply this same principle to every event of our lives, because each experience we encounter presents us with the classic Biblical choice between life or death, a blessing or a curse. To choose life, to choose blessing, to choose love and healing over death, darkness, and damnation is ultimately to choose God. For when you live in love, the gospel says, you live in God.

> ⚘ To choose life, to choose blessing, to choose love and healing over death, darkness, and damnation is ultimately to choose God.

Building up resentment

It's not just the big things that cause heartache and suffering in our lives. Little things can build up over time, and before long we may find ourselves in a constant state of low-level stress that can ruin our health and our relationships.

The one thing that annoyed Lydia about her husband Fred was the way he laughed. He'd giggle away at something funny like everybody else, but then at the end of his laugh, he'd inhale through his nose in a way that sounded like a straw sucking up the last drops of soda in a large cup. Actress Sandra Bullock sometimes employs this sound as a comic device for one of her more inelegant characters. But Fred did it naturally, and it bothered Lydia no end. She didn't say anything because she didn't want to hurt her husband's feelings, but every time she heard that snorking sound it rankled her.

Over time her resentment toward Fred grew. It wasn't that he did anything so terrible. It's just that Lydia's irritation had a cumulative effect. She started a mental catalogue of his "Snorking Offenses" and added to it daily. She began to snap at him for inconsequential things, and a "passive aggression" crept into their relationship. She avoided witty exchanges with him and wouldn't laugh at his little jokes, all because she didn't want to hear that sound.

It finally occurred to Lydia that her petty annoyance was beginning to trouble their relationship. Her affection toward Fred was beginning to cool, and they didn't have the fun together they used to have. She realized she needed to talk with her husband. She needed to let him off the hook and get over her dislike of the way he laughed. And maybe, just maybe, Fred might be able exercise a little control over the sound he made when he was having fun.

Sometimes couples, family members, co-workers and classmates don't attend to the little annoyances that might plague otherwise good relationships. But when we don't make a real effort to confront and forgive, and to change the way we behave, we run the risk of ramping up the negative energy that can ruin a good friendship, a good marriage, or a good job.

The forbidden anger

When things go wrong big-time, we may also get mighty angry at God. After all, it's God's job to deliver us from evil. How are we supposed to feel when God lets us slip into a tragedy without even a little warning? When a parent, spouse, or child suffers and dies, or a baby is born that will require intense care for the rest of its life, or a loved one becomes sick, or some other misfortune befalls us in a particularly nasty way, we may direct our resentment at God.

But anger against God puts us in a conundrum. Isn't it a sin to be angry with God? Won't that earn us even *more* trouble? How can we pray to God, or worship God, or be blessed by God if we're in a snit over how God is running our lives? Rather than risk retribution from God, we'll often simply repress our anger, bury it beneath layers of rationalization and denial so it doesn't show and perhaps isn't even felt.

The result of this kind of repression is a spiritual life that goes flat. Church loses its appeal and we begin to attend sporadically or stop going altogether. Prayer time dwindles and then fades. The Bible gets put away and begins to collect dust. We suffer because we're disconnecting ourselves from God. And God suffers, too. After all, God is love, and unrequited love must cause some form of divine heartache. The popular Catholic image of the Sacred Heart of Jesus helps us to appreciate this: It's a heart on fire with ardent love, yet painfully pierced with the thorns of rejection.

Better to have it out with God than to allow this essential relationship to wither. A spiritual director or pastoral minister can help during these times of animosity toward God. At some point, even God may need to be forgiven.

Thy will be done

Have you ever noticed that when something really good happens, like discovering gold on your property, people say, "Aren't you lucky"? But when something really bad happens, like an earthquake knocking down your house or a flood washing away your car, your insurance adjustor calls that an "act of God." It seems God often gets a bad rap.

We sometimes think that God runs the world like a magic

show, producing rabbits from a hat as needed. Worse still, we may also get the impression that God inflicts terrible things on us out of divine whim. For instance, when someone close to us dies unexpectedly, well-meaning people will try to comfort us by saying things like, "It must have been God's will" or "God must've had a reason." Perhaps it would surprise us to learn that God's will and God's intentions were not directly involved. God's ultimate will is on the record as taking a back seat to human will, even suffering the limitations of human weakness.

The stories in the Bible illustrate the point. From the first episode of God's interaction with humanity, the divine will is foiled by human weakness. God intended Adam and Eve to be happy in the Garden created for them. How did that work out? Not so hot. In the next story, God willed that the brothers Cain and Abel get along. The same question applies: How did that work out? And so on. When you think about it, God's will is hardly ever accomplished in the Bible. So what makes us think God's will is being done when somebody we love dies a tragic death or misfortune befalls an entire community?

The Bible does say that God limited the life span of human beings to seventy or eighty years—at least long enough to see our grandchildren. But human imperfections have a way of thwarting that design. Somebody decides to drive his car after he's had a few drinks and somebody else's life ends early. Or war breaks out because one nation is unwilling to coexist peacefully with its neighbors, and millions of people get killed. Imperfections can show up in a person's body in the form of diabetes or cancer or a birth defect, and life again comes up short. Many of God's beloved children die in the womb—some by the choice of their parents—and don't even get to see the light of day.

The impact of human imperfection on the world can be

devastating. People ask why God allows children to die of malnutrition and preventable diseases in places like Sudan, Haiti, and Bangladesh. In reality, God doesn't "allow" them to die at all. God clearly instructs people of faith to feed the hungry and provide for the needy. That they—or we—fail to do so surely can't be blamed on God.

One of the earliest things we learn from our religion is that God—and only God—is perfect. That means the rest of us are not perfect. So unless we want God to make everybody like little robots that have no freedom and can't make meaningful choices, we're stuck with the implications of human imperfection.

All of which means that, sooner or later, we've got to let God off the hook. God is trying to provide the grace, guidance, and instruction necessary for us to successfully live out our humanity. But all too often, it just doesn't work out the way we—or God—wants. In a sense, we need to forgive God. After all, God made us free to love as we are loved and to care for others the way God cares for us.

Conclusion

At times we can find it very difficult to forgive because the lessons of forgiveness are rarely taught and demonstrated during our upbringing. For the most part, the society around us operates on a system of reward-and-punishment, a system we buy into early. When people offend us, we tend to want to offend them back. We catalogue and maintain the offenses of others and keep them bound to their misdeeds. Carrying grudges tends to stress our nerves and take away our peace. When we hold God to the same standard we use to judge ourselves and others, we run the risk of becoming separated from the very source of love, healing, and hope. To reclaim our health and well-being, as well as the pleasure of family and friendships, we need to forgive God, ourselves, and one another, and join with God in the way of wholeness and peace.

What Do I Do When I Am Ready to Forgive?

"To forgive oneself"—? No, that doesn't work; we have to be forgiven. But we can only believe this is possible if we ourselves can forgive. — Dag Hammarskjöld

First-century Greek essayist Plutarch told the story of a man who wanted to make a dead body stand up. The determined man tried everything—balancing the corpse, experimenting with various postures—but none of his attempts were successful. In the end the man was forced to throw up his hands and admit the truth: "There is something missing on the inside."

If we make the choice to live without forgiveness, we may find ourselves in the same circumstance as that unfortunate corpse. Without forgiveness, something vital is missing from our relationships with God, with ourselves, and with others. The work of forgiveness is not merely a necessary component to relationship; it may be the reason we humans are given to one another in the first place. As the founder of the l'Arche communities Jean Vanier wrote in his insightful book *Community and Growth: Our Pilgrimage Together*: "If we come into community without knowing that the reason we come is to discover the mystery of forgiveness, we will soon be disappointed."

Anyone who has ever lived in a household of more than one knows the truth of that statement. The very act of forming relationships invites us into the mystery of otherness. When another enters our lives, we seek out what makes us alike, but we soon also run up against our differences as well. Will we reject what is unlike us or seek to understand and respect it, maybe even come to appreciate it? Vanier also notes, "Forgiveness and celebration...are the two faces of love." Learning to love, then, involves moving through times of conflict to the ever-awaiting hour of celebration.

In order to explore the mystery of forgiveness and the role of celebration, it might be helpful to back-pedal for a brief look at where forgiveness comes from—which is, theologically speaking, from the occasion of human failing.

That unfashionable word "sin"

Back when it was in fashion to scrutinize the now-ascendant Generation X, endless questionnaires were compiled in an attempt to capture the essence of the society that would one day replace that of the WWII generation and the Baby Boomers. In one of those studies, it was discovered that many of those born in the 1960s and '70s categorically rejected the notion of sin. The word that had once held great power and emotional wallop for their parents and their grandparents was, for Gen X, a curiously empty term. It was as if the very idea of a religiously defined evil had exited the room. What replaced it, if anything, was a morality based on a nebulous sense of "what's right." All too often, this simply became shorthand for "what's right for me."

At least part of the Gen X rejection of time-honored concepts like evil and sin had to do with the over-employment of those terms by previous generations. In the past, sin apparently was everywhere—under every rock and behind every tree. It became identified as the source of whatever misfortune might be out there. The notion of evil had degenerated, basically, into whatever grownups were most afraid of. All too often, that meant sin was coupled with sexuality and matters regarding procreation. The backlash to this simultaneous overextension and narrow usage was to render the terms obsolete, if not ludicrous. One of the unfortunate consequences of sin's departure from the conversation was a gap in the ability to talk meaningfully about forgiveness. Like the dead body that won't stand up, something is missing in our understanding of forgiveness if, from the outset, we don't "believe" in sin.

So let's lay some groundwork to reconstruct a healthy Catholic understanding of sin and evil. The theological backdrop for the concept of sin is the Hebrew word *hamar*, which means "missing the mark." When an archer shoots an arrow that flies past the bull's-eye by inches or even yards, we would not think to call that inaccuracy sinful. But the image at the root of the Hebrew word for sin helps us to appreciate that in the Judeo-Christian worldview there is a target, something we ought to be aiming at with our actions, decisions, and relationships. Described in a word, that bull's-eye is love. "God is love," says the Scripture, and when we miss that mark, by a little or a lot, the inaccuracy is often measured in terms of human suffering.

Sometimes we simply fail to love; that's known as a *sin of omission*. Sometimes we actively choose to do harm; that would be a *sin of commission*. Common acts of omission include withholding the truth, not being generous, listening to gossip without objection, and neglecting the call to justice. In each instance, we "omit" love from the equation. Sins of commission include the more dynamic forms of wrongdoing: stealing, lying, cheating, injustice, all the way up to acts of violence. Here we "commit" actions—and commit ourselves to a course—clearly opposed to the way of love.

In the tradition of the church, sin is defined not only by the nature of our involvement (active commission or passive omission), but also by the degree of the offense. Venial sin concerns a matter of less consequence and is often thoughtlessly carried out or stumbled into. Serious sin is known as *mortal* because it effectively endangers the spiritual viability of the person committing it. For an act to be considered a mortal sin, it has to meet three conditions: It must be deliberately chosen, involve a grave matter, and be entered into with full understanding of its consequences. For example, tying an antagonist to the railroad tracks before the scheduled arrival of a train would be a mortal sin; arguing with an antagonist who, distracted, steps onto the tracks and into the path of an oncoming train would not.

All of these ways of defining our culpability in wrongdoing highlight the perception that sin is, by its nature, antisocial. In the Bible, Genesis describes in story form the advent of sin as a fundamental experience of alienation. Originally, creation is in union with its Creator, and man and woman are in harmony with each other and with the garden they tend. But the choice for sin at once divides humanity from its God and the two human partners from each other. Adam accuses Eve; Eve blames the creature; both hide from God. In the same way, sin results in creation's interior disunity. Now working the land will be by the sweat of our brow and bearing children will cause suffering. Original harmony has disintegrated into endless waves of division, antagonism, and struggle. The loving unity that was intended has become a chaotic battlefield of defended turf and narrow self-interest.

☙ All of these ways of defining our culpability in wrongdoing highlight the perception that sin is, by its nature, antisocial.

The atmosphere of alienation passes to the next generation. Cain kills his brother and lies to God about it. Cain also fears retribution at the hands of others. In a few more generations, the world is rife with evil and the experiment of creation appears to be, by all measures, an utter failure. God resolves to wash the earth clean and start over, rescuing a remnant of the original creation in Noah's family and the other inhabitants of the ark. Even this drastic maneuver does not rid the world of sin, however. Before long, the reestablished community is severed by language and the spirit of nationalism at the Tower of Babel. Now, it seems, human beings can't even *talk* to each other anymore, much less live together as one people. The environment of alienation has become the very definition of the society that human hands have made.

The Catholic Church does not interpret the stories of Genesis to be a literal history of the beginning of time. But the church does embrace these stories as the wisdom of the ages, the revelation of God, and instructive in our understanding of what went wrong and what continues to go wrong in humanity's relationship with God, creation, and one another. Sin would later be further codified in the great list of Ten Commandments, which outlines the major categories of human offense. But even without the list, the destructive quality of sin could not be more evident. Humanity's need for outside help to overcome the consequence of all this alienation is also plain. Enter Jesus of Nazareth.

What to do with sin?

Some forms of sin that come down the pike can definitely be avoided by deliberate human decision. The fact that we are confronted with an "occasion of sin" doesn't mean we have to capitulate to it. The married person can choose not to have an affair with the beautiful stranger, for example, or the CEO does not have to make a profit at the expense of the environment. But we are not simply tempted toward isolated sinful choices; we are at the same time immersed in the ongoing reality of sin, what Saint Augustine dubbed *original sin*. Augustine's idea is that sin is the result of disobedience. The word *obedience* has its roots in hearing or listening; theological disobedience means we're not listening clearly to the One whose word is the source of life itself. Once humanity stopped listening, the possibility of "missing the mark"—the definition of sin—fatefully entered creation. Our reality became indelibly tainted with it. Once generated, sin is now a moral cancer that replicates and spreads with great initiative and efficiency. Though each of us may duck many or even most occasions of sin that come our way, the pervasive conditions that sin inaugurated in our world are here to stay: They are like the holes of miscalculation left by many an arrow that landed far from the bull's-eye.

In this sense, then, humanity is stuck with the global conditions that make for poverty and social injustice. Around the world, the human deck of fortune and misfortune continues to be shuffled and dealt most unevenly. Even if we humans were all on our best behavior all the time, conflict appears to be inevitable. The fact is, of course, most of us are not on our best behavior much of the time, and widespread evil is the result.

The story of Noah and his ark offers the hopeful insight that God is not planning to destroy the world in order to save it. God's renewed covenant with Noah included people and animals alike in a divine pledge of sustenance. But the need to mop up the mess created by human history still persists. God's mercy remains the janitor of choice in both the Hebrew and Christian Scriptures. In the Christian story, Jesus becomes the embodiment of that mercy, the very word of God's compassion made flesh. Throughout the New Testament, the Christian presumption—and it is a great and daring presumption—is that God's forgiveness is a free gift, neither deserved because of our goodness nor earned through the sincerity of our repentance. Forgiveness isn't something we have to talk God into doing. As Jesus announced from the cross in John's gospel, "It is accomplished." All we have to do is embrace it.

How do we accept forgiveness?

Catholic Christians have a formal process for embracing the God-given reality of forgiveness known as the *Sacrament of Reconciliation*. (It is also variously called Penance or Confession.) The sacrament is probably the most frequently caricatured and most poorly understood ritual of the church. Many think Catholics believe that only a Catholic priest can forgive sins or that telling sins to a priest is somehow necessary for God to hear them or to accept our regrets. This is not accurate.

Colonial author Nathaniel Hawthorne, a lifelong Puritan,

had a better perception of the sacrament than many Catholics do. Steeped in a culture of shame, accusation, and condemnation, Hawthorne spent his career writing stories about what happens to the human heart locked into tormenting cycles of guilt. Yet the author of *The Scarlet Letter* confided that he wished he were a Catholic for one reason: in order to approach the confessional and be absolved of his sin. It was the confidence of the sacrament that Hawthorne admired, the idea that, through the ritual itself, the sinner was assured that the damage caused by one's sins stopped at the door of the confessional box. In the Sacrament of Reconciliation, human guilt had an outlet and embraced the certainty of God's mercy.

This is what it means to approach the sacrament: not that sins are forgiven *because* of the ritual but that through the ritual we receive the *assurance* of the forgiveness of sin and have the opportunity to commit to the new possibilities inherent in God's mercy. Reconciliation is the church's way of celebrating a gift God alone can bestow.

While Catholic rituals of forgiveness may be free, they are never cheap. Archbishop Fulton Sheen noted that you can't imitate the ritual elements of the Sacrament of Reconciliation piecemeal and come up with a facsimile result. In his book *Peace of Soul*, Sheen observed, "A few decades ago, nobody believed in the confession of sins except the Church. Today everyone believes in confession, with this difference: Some believe in confessing their own sins; others believe in confessing other people's sins." Though he was writing in the 1950s, Sheen's assessment still has a surprisingly contemporary sound. "Outing" the behavior of others will not move us closer to the spirit of forgiveness. If we approach the sacrament in order to exonerate ourselves with explanations and extenuating circumstances, we are getting the ritual wrong. If we hope to point the finger of blame at someone else, a phone call to a radio talk show would serve better than the confessional. Getting the elements of the forgiveness ritual right is basic to achieving the results of the process.

So let's examine the five stages of forgiveness as celebrated in the Catholic Sacrament of Reconciliation to see how they promote the process of embracing and incorporating God's mercy. We might call them the Five C's of reconciliation: Conviction, Confession, Contrition, Compensation, and Correction.

Conviction: I have done wrong

From news reports of the last decade, it is all too easy to recall the emphatic denials of guilt our public leaders routinely make. Presidents, governors, congressional representatives and civic leaders of every rank have stood up before the cameras and told us that—whatever the offense was—they didn't do it, they weren't responsible, there were mitigating circumstances, and they didn't have all the information needed at the time to make better choices. Business and industry leaders have made the same protestations before their board members and in front of judges. Religious authorities have denied responsibility, closed their files, paid off potential troublemakers, and refused to admit any wrongdoing.

It may be difficult, in fact, to recall any examples of people in public life who did wrong and said so, unless you go all the way back to George Washington and his cherry tree. The old-fashioned principle of examining one's conscience and accepting personal responsibility has all but vanished from the modern scene. In order to seek forgiveness, we first have to admit that we have done wrong. We have to "convict ourselves" of surrendering to sinful impulses and choosing a direction that misses the mark of love. (If some Catholics have been unable to accept the apologies of American bishops in response to the damage done in the clergy abuse scandals, it is because few bishops have admitted that they too have sinned.)

🌿 **Owning responsibility for what we have done or failed to do is not easy.**

Let's be clear about what convicting ourselves entails. We can't make evasive assertions ("Wrong has been done." "Mistakes were made.") Nor can we rush into self-justification ("I did spread the rumor, but only because it seemed plausible at the time, and it was from a reliable source.") And above all, we can't seek to exonerate ourselves by shifting or sharing the blame. ("Yes, I was unfaithful, but so was he." "I haven't shown charity to the disadvantaged, but I don't give money to the poor because they just spend it on booze.")

Owning responsibility for what we have done or failed to do is not easy. Our reflex is to protect ourselves from the discomfort of guilt by assigning blame to others as quickly as possible. In the reward-and-punishment system in which we were schooled, clearing ourselves and blaming others was a necessary form of self-defense.

This is why, for example, it took Justin nearly two decades to accept the reason he was unable to retain a job for more than a season. Justin was fired early and often, but it was never his fault. His first boss, he asserted, was an alcoholic. The boss would get liquored up, fire Justin, and then rehire him after becoming sober enough to realize he couldn't run the business without him. When Justin finally got tired of being a human yo-yo, he moved on to another employer, who treated all the workers in the warehouse as if they were under-producing farm animals or machines that needed a kick once in a while to perform. Each subsequent position Justin took seemed to follow an eerie pattern: an impossible work environment featuring a tyrannical or irrational boss. Was it Justin's fault that he simply couldn't work for these jerks for more than six months?

After twenty years of being hired and fired or just quitting when the conflict got too high, it occurred to Justin that the one consistent factor in each circumstance in his life was—himself. Up to now he had been concentrating on the failings of the people around him, which were undoubtedly considerable. But on the night of his latest dismissal, as he sat alone with his dinner, all at once the thought bobbed up that he would not like to have himself as an employee either. The implications of that admission flooded him like chards of revelation. Whether or not his bosses had been fair or smart or reasonable, he himself was not an ideal person to work with. Once Justin turned the idea over in his mind and accepted it, it was not so scary. His work history replayed before him like a whole new story about someone else. Obviously, there was another way to look at the revolving door of his employment history besides blaming it all on "those jerks" he had worked for. It was a perspective considerably less flattering to himself, but more truthful. Justin resolved to stop recounting the story of his life in terms of how badly he'd been treated by those in authority over him. Instead, he'd look to the future and concentrate on being the best man he could be on the next jobsite. In large part because of his new attitude, the next job he took turned out to be the last one he ever had. He retired from there recently after thirty years of service.

Being "convicted by the truth" about ourselves can seem like a minor death experience, particularly if we are not used to being honest with ourselves about who we are. If the notion that we are sinners is foreign to us, or if we have spent a lifetime keeping personal responsibility at bay, the truth about ourselves may seem too awful to bear all in a moment. Yet once we understand that hiding from the truth consigns us to a prison of lifelong self-deception, we may be grateful to be handed the key to liberty at last. As Jesus put it, "You shall know the truth, and the truth shall set you free."

Confession: I reveal my offense

Accepting that we have done wrong and are capable of being wrongdoers is the first necessary step toward forgiveness. It seems obvious, but we cannot be forgiven if we persist in the belief that we have done nothing wrong. Otherwise, what's to forgive?

Once we own our culpability, the next step is to say it aloud to someone else. This public confession is not for the purpose of embarrassment or punishment. Technically speaking, we've already embarrassed ourselves plenty by making the choice to do wrong. Bringing the offense out of hiding is important in order to stand by our reclaimed self-knowledge. It achieves the same purpose as having a godparent at a christening or a witness at a wedding. Public acknowledgment of a promise binds us all to uphold the pledge. In the case of personal confession, we are binding ourselves to the truth and ensuring that we can't back out later, change our minds, and re-adopt the lie.

As we noted in the brief biblical overview of Genesis stories, sin is an antisocial event. It ruptures our relationships with God, ourselves, and others. In order to mend such a breech, it makes sense to involve others, or at least one community representative, in the process of restoration. In the sacramental practice of reconciliation, the chosen confessor stands in for both

God and the community that has suffered the offense.

In some circumstances, secular rituals of forgiveness will more appropriately involve seeking out the person we have offended as the one to receive our confession of wrongdoing. Without being too dramatic about the whole thing, this is what we normally do anyway. Say you close a door in someone's face thoughtlessly. From whom do you beg pardon? Few of us would turn to a bystander at random and apologize! In the same way, when we have a blowup with a family member, we often work our way toward a direct expression of "I'm sorry" even before the argument has ended. Admitting responsibility and asking for forgiveness on the spot is the best way to proceed in any circumstance of offense. But we don't always do that because of shame, pride, fear, or denial. The more time passes, the longer the list of grievances can grow and the harder it can be to own up to our culpability.

A recent article in the newspaper described an "apology hotline" operating in New York. It was designed to be a strictly anonymous affair: callers could dial up and get whatever burdened them off their chests, without fear of judgment or reprisals. All confessions to the hotline were delivered to the cool medium of an answering machine. Some called to admit embezzlement, lying, or cheating on spouses. Others addressed their apologies as if to the offended parties and then asked for something in return: purification, closure, release from the pangs of guilt. Like a stone Buddha with closed eyes, the answering machine kept its own counsel in utter silence. It is hard to know if the fifty or so weekly callers got what they were looking for. The apology hotline differs significantly from the sacramental ritual of confession in that no one is on the other side to take the call. According to the article, the caller's confession is played back later by a college student who set up the service. The student remains hopeful that the act of confessing will in itself prove helpful to people. But since there is no genuine exchange between persons, the admission of responsibility melts into an unfortunately sterile void, like a note in a bottle cast out to sea.

Genuine ritual confession requires a bit more courage than calling the hotline. Even in the old-style Catholic confessional box, with its heavy curtains and sliding wooden screens preserving anonymity, there was still the breathtaking moment of actually giving voice to what you had done, knowing full well that the priest was on the other side of the screen ready to respond to your words. In the decades since the Second Vatican Council of the 1960's, the ritual of the confessional has largely given way to a face-to-face encounter in a small room. There, confessor and penitent honestly confront the embarrassingly antisocial nature of sin and the profoundly social nature of grace. Together, they explore what has been done and what can be done to promote healing and hope for the future.

✻ In genuine ritual confession, two persons honestly confront the embarrassingly antisocial nature of sin and the profoundly social nature of grace.

More recently, the communal celebration of the Sacrament of Reconciliation has become popular. This practice has the advantage of recognizing the social nature of sin: It is because of "what we have done and what we have failed to do," the community suffers. The communal celebration, however, always includes the opportunity for individual confession to a priest, a necessary component in the case of mortal sin.

Contrition: I express sorrow

When most of us manage to louse up our relationships, as we often do, we are plenty sorry on the spot. We feel regret about a lot of things: words we said that will be hard to take back, decisions we made that will be complicated to undo. We deeply regret that there's a mess to clean up, not to mention all the uncomfortable feelings generated that have to be dealt with on the other side of conflict. We may be sorry as a sad-eyed hound dog about all these things, but that's not the same thing as contrition.

When we are completely honest, we admit that much of the time the remorse we feel for initiating conflict and division is really no more than feeling sorry for ourselves for having gotten into a situation. Our regret is no more than wishing away the consequences of our poor choices. But sometimes the look of pain on the face of a loved one is enough to make us feel genuine sorrow for being the source of harm. The anguish of isolation caused by secret acts of betrayal can cut so deeply that we sincerely want the burden of shame to be lifted and the sadness borne away. In these moments, the lively sense of sorrow we experience approaches the condition of sacramental contrition. When we bring this sorrow forward and speak it out loud, we admit that the damage we have done cuts both ways: with ourselves and with others.

Sixteen-year-old Maria had a stormy relationship with her father. Mostly there were seasons of icy silence between them, followed by outbursts of strong and mutual hostility. One night as Maria returned home, she sensed by the mood of the rest of the family that trouble was in the air. It was not long before her father stomped into the room and began hurling accusations and insults her way. Maria's desire to scream back at him was immense within her. This was how the evening was scripted to go, as per their long and bitter custom. But on that particular night, she also felt the uselessness of another hour spent nurturing hatred. The legacy of this antagonism was nothing but hurt for him, for her, and for her mother, brothers and sisters as well. Maria wanted all the unhappiness to stop; she was desperate to put an end to it, and she was—in a word—sorry for her part in it.

Before she knew what she was saying, Maria shouted across the room at her father: "No matter what you say, I know you love me!" The surprising accusation seemed to hit the enraged man in the chest like bullets. He staggered slightly, and stopped shouting. Then he stammered back, helplessly, "And I always know, Maria, that you love me."

❧ **Contrition is important in the work of forgiveness, because it lays bare the heart. It creates vulnerability and access, and is an invitation to love.**

Maria cried as she opened her arms to the man who had been her accuser only moments ago. Like a needy child, her father fell into her embrace, and they wept together. The whole family stood stunned and in awe in the presence of a domestic miracle. There would not be another night of shouting between Maria and her father again. The relationship would never be easy, heaven knows, but a new path of possibility opened for them that night.

Contrition is important in the work of forgiveness, because it lays bare the heart. It creates vulnerability and access, and is an invitation to love. Since love is the main casualty in our choice for sin, our ability to reconnect with the source of love is vital for rebuilding the bridge to hope and new life. If we dearly want things to change, if we are finally ready and willing to change ourselves, a lively sorrow for our sins is the one sure passage into a new place.

Compensation: I fix what I broke

In some ways we might say that the thief gets off the easiest in the confessional. All he or she has to do is return what was taken to pay back the debt; it can even be done anonymously. But what if what was stolen was someone's good name? How can that be restored? Or what if the offense is a broken heart? What glue can be used to fix it? What if the injury committed is very old, and the person offended is now lost to the past or deceased? What then can be done to heal the damage?

The task of compensation can seem like the most arduous and uncertain step on the road to forgiveness. We have to remind ourselves that according to Christian theology our forgiveness doesn't *depend* on our earning it by some achievement of our own. God forgives by divine initiative, and the reconciliation of sinners is already accomplished through the compassion of Jesus Christ. As Saint Paul might say, the price demanded by sin is death, but that debt has already been paid at the cross.

So in terms of sacramental forgiveness, nothing we do makes us *worthy* to be forgiven, and there are no requirements to fill that would *force* God to remit forgiveness. God forgives us, in other words, because we have sinned and *need* to be forgiven. Our need is the only qualification God is looking for.

The sacramental steps we have taken toward reconciliation so far—Conviction, Confession, Contrition—are for the purpose of awakening us to the need for forgiveness and opening us to the possibility of receiving it into our lives. These steps do not make us eligible for forgiveness, nor do they pay our way into God's good graces. But through these steps, we find ourselves prepared to incorporate the reality of forgiveness into our lives and admit the hope of healing and peace. Without these first three steps, forgiveness often remains a wrapped and forgotten gift, undiscovered and unable to release its promise. But it is compensation that moves us out of feelings and words and into the world of action. Forgiveness, after all, is not an emotional experience; it is closer to what the Buddhists mean by "right relationship."

A soldier tells the story of becoming discouraged on the battlefield. The endless days of violence endured and violence committed had reduced him to something less than human. He felt he had a heart like stone. Just when he was beginning to contemplate suicide as the only way out of this hell, a small group of stragglers emerged from a long-term hiding place in the hills above the soldier's camp. They were the enemy, to be sure, but also they were a family of children, women, and old men. And they were starving. The soldier knew that his commanding officer might demand that these people be killed, incarcerated, or at the least ignored. But he determined instead to feed them. Compared with the atrocities of war, this act of compensation was insignificant. It did, however, save the soldier's life, not to mention the lives of one small family.

Compensation works as a means of balancing the debt of injury in the world and also as a way of delivering us from the aftereffects of sin: the crusting, bruising, de-humanizing aspects of our own wrongdoing. When we choose sin, we choose against love, which is another way of saying we choose against our own nature, since we are made in the image of a God who is love. Sin denies and defaces that image in us; compensation helps chisel away the barnacles left by sin so we may emerge once more with the face of love intact.

Sometimes it's simple to fix what we broke by our offense. We can go back and speak the truth; offer an apology; replace what was lost; mend the tattered relationship. Sometimes there is still time for second chances and revised good intentions. But even when a particular situation is broken beyond repair, we can still make compensation in other ways. The former junkie may not be able to reclaim the lives affected by the drugs he sold and the family he estranged, but he can speak to schoolchildren about the dead-end route of crime and addiction and thereby prevent more harm from being done. A marriage may end in divorce, but the lessons learned by both parties can lead to better, healthier partnerships in the future. A troubled relationship with a parent may not have been resolved before death took one of the participants. But we can pray for the deceased, wish them peace, forgive them their trespasses, and ask forgiveness for our own. In these and many other ways, the cycle of sin can be broken, the damage caused by sin can be healed, and the work of mercy can flow forward through the very channels our offenses once moved.

Correction: I resolve for the future

Any one of us, if caught in the right circumstances, might find ourselves capable of committing a "crime of passion." Our sympathies are therefore available to those who are buoyed along by a wave of emotional events that lead to tragic results. But we have less compassion for the methodical serial killer, the chronic adulterer, the abuser of power, or the habitual liar. Because we know the contents of our own hearts, we know that people sometimes make bad choices. When they make the same choices again and again, however, we doubt their good will and increase their moral culpability.

The will to amend our lives, or correction, is the natural final step in incorporating the healing power of forgiveness and integrating it into our being. The Catholic approach to forgiveness says we must not only mend the breech of the past but also construct a bridge into the future. The resolve to correct our behavior from now on is a key part of the forgiveness process.

A popular prayer used in the Catholic Sacrament of Reconciliation puts it this way: "I firmly resolve, with the help of Thy grace, to sin no more and to avoid the near occasion of sin."

A pledge to sin no more? Is it reasonable, given the reality of human weakness, to take such a pledge? Is it possible to keep it? Humanly, no; by the definition of original sin, we are all suspended in the soup of mortal sinfulness and subject to the sorry human condition for as long as we live. Being of free will, however, we can also make strong decisions not to sin in particular circumstances and to avoid "occasions" that lead to sin: drunkenness, which weakens our judgment; too much stress, which makes us weak and vulnerable; the companionship of inveterate gamblers or cheaters or cynics, who make it seem cool to join their ranks. But the one thing we cannot honestly do is promise not to sin again. That, humanly speaking, is beyond us. But it is not beyond God, who supplies the grace necessary for us to amend our lives.

Even those who join recovery programs do not swear off their addictions forever—only "for today." Today is a manageable mortal piece to stake our claim on. Biting off more than today could choke us on infinity. The prayer of contrition is not a pledge to swear off sin forever, not even a particular sin. What we say is "I firmly resolve"—I make it my absolute intention—not to choose sin over love. We further say that this resolve will be carried out "with the help of Thy grace"—through the entirely capable power of God's strength, not our own. This is a significant point, for a permanent change of heart and direction can only be achieved if we rely on God for help. Human will alone has historically proven itself to be a frail and fallible thing.

With the resolve to correct our lives, we come full circle in the acceptance of forgiveness. We acknowledge that we—not someone else—did wrong. We are willing to admit our guilt openly. We have experienced sorrow for our actions and opened our hearts to the way of love once more. We seek to regain our human-ity, lost in turning away from love, by engaging in loving acts that seek to restore the balance and contrib-ute to the healing of injury. Finally, we want to begin again and choose a new way. We ask for the grace to be guided and guarded as we make these tentative steps down a new path.

> ❧ Permanent change of heart and direction can only be achieved if we rely on God for help.

Doug found out about correction after one of his famous parties. He was a popular guy, everybody's best friend, dedicated to showing the world a good time. After an evening spent entertaining his closest pals, he felt really "up" about his ability to bring people together. The food, the music, the conversation had all been superb. He was sure people would be talking about that gathering for some time to come. "Where Doug is," he liked to say, "the fun begins!"

Imagine how shocked and deflated he was when one of those friends called him the next day and said, "Doug, it's really awful the way you monopolized the conversation last night. Every time someone told a story, you had to tell a better one. Not everybody has an exciting, colorful life like yours. You ought to give some thought to how other people feel when you try to come off as being ten times more interesting than they are."

Doug was wounded, and his first impulse was to dismiss this warning as the grumbling of some boring, jealous dude. But as the months passed and social occasions piled up, he had the opportunity to watch himself in action—and it wasn't pretty. He heard himself doing it: trumping people, one-upping every tall tale, competing for center stage, crushing all comers by being funnier, smarter, more practiced in the art of table talk. With a grimace, Doug watched as shyer, less confident, less verbally gifted folk were threatened, harmed, and finally silenced by his mow-down-the-opposition approach to conversation.

Finally, Doug could stand himself no longer as he observed a timid woman open her mouth to speak for the third time and then shrink back when he resumed his fiercely witty monologue. He interrupted himself. "And what about you?" he managed to say, fixing his eyes on the woman and offering his kindest smile. "Let's hear from someone intelligent for a change!" Laughter broke out around the table, and the conversational baton finally exchanged hands.

Doug still throws the best parties, and he is undeniably a funny guy. But he has added compassion and empathy to his arsenal of good traits, and he has more friends where fans and admirers used to be. He corrected his behavior and completed the process of reconciliation.

Conclusion

These five ritual steps toward forgiveness are more like a circle than a staircase. We arrive where we began: in the knowledge and absolute assurance that our forgiveness is already achieved. But in the ritual of forgiveness, what is achieved is fully received. The gift has been given, and we have opened it and discovered its substance and value. With hearts full of gratitude, we embrace the Giver and feel once more loved and affirmed in our relationship. Imbued with the spirit of thankfulness, we can share what we have received with others.

The Practice of Forgiving

When it is possible to speak a word, it liberates.
We do not always remember that it is precisely a word,
a Word articulated in our flesh, which has liberated us.
— Pierre Wolff

The Catholic concept of forgiveness is not merely a nice idea. It's a way of life for those who believe. But where does our concept of forgiveness come from? How did it develop? And why is it that we have to forgive?

We return once more to the Garden of Genesis, the way detectives keep circling back to the crime scene. The creation story has been our starting point for understanding human freedom, as well as for exploring the alienation that results from choosing not to listen to the source of life and love. Here, we want to use the terms of the story to consider why the choice for sin is so grotesque and its consequences so apparently outsized and disastrous. As the story goes, God set up Adam and Eve in a perfect world where they could have everything they wanted in an endless existence of pure bliss. There was only one rule: they couldn't eat the fruit from the tree of the knowledge of good and evil. In other words, they had to trust all judgment to God and accept divine perfection for what it is. Not a bad deal, considering who it was they were working with.

But they broke the rule anyway and introduced disobedience into their otherwise sinless existence. It was then no longer possible for these now imperfect people to remain in the perfect life of the Garden. So, out into the world they went where they would experience the consequences of their imperfection: toil and frustration, hardship, suffering and death.

Considering the immense collateral damage involved in their choice, we have to ask ourselves: Was this God punishing them for breaking the rules? Well, that's one way of looking at it, and it's been a popular one in our reward-and-punishment-oriented religious history and practice. But suppose your mother imposed a rule on you that said, "Thou shalt not play in the street." And suppose you broke that rule and ran after your ball into the street. And suppose a steamroller came along and squashed you flat. Would that be your mother punishing you for breaking her rule? Was it she who sent the steamroller to smite you for your disobedience? Or would your two-dimensional end simply be the unfortunate consequence of your failure to comprehend the tremendous love and care your mother had for you and her great concern for your safety and well-being? Would it not also indicate the wisdom she possessed about streets and steamrollers and the danger that awaits a not-so-smart child who ventures beyond the sidewalk?

In the same way, stories of human imperfection and the natural consequences that arise from them chart a painful course through the Old Testament. Cain killed his brother Abel and had to live the rest of his life alienated from his family. Like your favorite gardening shirt that finally gets so dirty that it goes in the laundry basket, the world became so evil that it needed a good flood to wash it clean. But that didn't stop the dirt from returning or even slow it down. Abraham, Isaac, and Jacob all told lies and were deceived in turn. Moses had a terrible temper that drove him at times to violence. It made him ineligible for the new way of the Promised Land. Samson broke the rules and played dangerous games against some pretty tough opponents and lost his freedom and his eyesight. David may have scored points when he slew Goliath with a rock between the eyes, but that business with Bathsheba involved murder and adultery and caused the great king a world of hurt. His son Solomon was famously wise, but not smart enough to listen to Rule #1: Don't worship false gods. He permitted such worship, and it divided his kingdom.

It helps to remember, when reciting these stories, that these are the *good* guys. Yet the steamroller of sin-and-consequence rolled over them all the same. The farther through biblical history you go, the worse it gets. Eventually the whole people of Israel were so far off the track that they were sent out of the room and into exile in Babylon. For generations, the prophets had been really clear with the leaders of Israel about political strategy and foreign policy. They delivered God's word of life in great detail; all the leaders had to do was listen. But worldly power and wealth provided too much temptation for the politicians—imagine that! They ignored the prophet's warnings and went the way that seemed best to them. Like the kid playing in the street against his mother's orders, the result is that Israel got run over by its enemies and packed off into captivity.

One way to talk about the whole biblical history is in terms of God's laws and divine punishments. Another way to view the story is that people got what they paid for. God may not have to go after us for our sins, it turns out, when the consequences of sin are often punishment enough.

The golden thread of redemption

So, where does the forgiveness part come in? After all, if you examine the stories of the Old Testament and keep track, just about every offense gets punished and every infraction has its penalty. Nobody gets away with anything.

But winding through these stories of punitive justice like a golden thread woven into a blanket of coarse wool is the hope of a new day, when God's mercy and forgiveness would lift the people above their faults and restore them to a life of security and peace. The prophet Ezekiel raised this proclamation in the voice of God: "I will sprinkle clean water upon you to cleanse you from all your impurities. I will give you a new heart and put my spirit within you. You shall be my people, and I will be your God."

"Though your sins are like scarlet," wrote the prophet Isaiah, "I will make them like snow."

The "performance prophet" Hosea said it a different way. He married a woman with the unfortunate name of Gomer. Though she constantly cheated on him, Hosea always begged her to come back, because he loved her so. In his role as prophet, he embraced the responsibility to demonstrate with his own marital situation the great love God had for his people and God's willingness, even ardent desire, to forgive everything his people had done and take them back as his beloved spouse.

Divine forgiveness was clearly the only release from the prison of human sinfulness, but how to achieve it? The people of Israel languished for a whole generation in Babylonian captivity in a kind of cosmic Catch-22. The ordinary means of escape from the effects of sin—atoning for their offenses by offering sacrifices in the Jerusalem temple—was not possible. Jerusalem was completely trashed and there was nothing left to the temple but a pile of rubble. So, Israel was up the creek, enslaved in Babylon till the end of time with no hope ... except for that one thread of gold: God's mercy and forgiveness.

If you were God, what do you do? Well, that's exactly what God did, according to the way the story is told. If you're the one who made the rules of the cosmos, you're also the one who can break them. Through an extraordinary, and totally unexpected series of events, Israel got turned loose and sent back home—with financial backing to rebuild their lives and start all over again no less. That was the beginning of a new season of faith for the people of God, who began to see their relationship with God very differently. They would carry the customs and traditions of this new hope into the Christian era.

Mercy becomes flesh

Jesus was the Christian embodiment of that new hope of Israel. He became the living, breathing, flesh-and-blood expression of God's mercy and compassion. Forgiveness flowed out from him gratuitously. Nobody had to earn it. Nobody even had to ask for it. Jesus told the paralyzed man that his sins were forgiven before he ever said a word. The woman caught in adultery was pardoned without confessing her sin or asking for forgiveness. All the woman with the hemorrhage had to do was sneak up behind him and touch the hem of his coat and healing power rushed from him into her.

It's important to understand that at the time Jesus walked the land, people believed that afflictions were the direct result of their own misdeeds. They were blind or lame or deaf or sick or possessed by an evil spirit because they had done something to deserve it. Their suffering was God was punishing them. Remember the question asked by the disciples when they encountered the man who was born blind? They wanted to know how it happened. Was it the man's own sin, somehow anticipated by his blindness at birth? (Maybe like Jacob and Esau, he did something in utero that got him in trouble.) Or maybe his parents committed some terrible sin that resulted in their son being born blind. And remember the Lord's answer: It was none of those things that caused his blindness.

❧ God isn't doing any of these things to us. God is trying to save us; that's what God does.

We need to take that to heart because, even in our modern age, we still tend to link our misfortunes with God's unrelenting justice. When tragedy befalls us, don't we often say, "What did I do to deserve this?" or "Why is God doing this to me?" Smoking may lead to cancer and heart disease, toxic work environments may cause illnesses of all kinds, stress may bring on high blood pressure, and overeating may send us to an early grave—but God isn't doing any of these things to us. God is trying to save us; that's what God does.

In his teaching, preaching, healing, and example, Jesus did what he could to break the popular understanding of the sin-punishment connection. In his final act, for the sake of the very people who rejected him, humiliated him, condemned him, whipped him, stripped him, drove nails into his hands, mocked him, spit on him and left him to die—for these people, Jesus prayed for God's forgiveness. They did not confess that they had done wrong, nor did they say they were sorry, nor did they ask for forgiveness. Jesus simply forgave them because it was in him to do that. He was the revelation of the mercy and love of God; he was what God is like. He was, we say, the *Son of God.*

Growing from law to grace

The story of the cross seems a long way from the story of the ancient flood. "Is this the same God?" people ask when they read both stories. It's not that God changed; people changed, as did their perspective on God and how they understood divine intentions. God remains constant in the divine self-revelation. But human understanding develops over time and more accurately discovers God's self-revelation piece by piece. Our progression in knowing God tends to follow the progression of human development overall. The primitive understanding of divinity was that God was a warrior leading his people into battle against their enemies. That image of God best fit the Hebrew tribal culture that had to constantly fight for its existence in an environment of hostility among other tribal cultures.

As the Hebrew people evolved from their ancient nomadic roots to become a settled urban and agricultural society, their relationship to God developed in tandem to become more social and liturgical in its scope. God's stable and reliable presence was woven into the stability of religious temple practices. God's instruction concerning how the people were to conduct their civil affairs and foreign policy fit their new role as a nation among nations.

At the same time, the earlier understanding of God as an exacting taskmaster, strict and uncompromising in justice—

traits necessary to keep a rag-tag tribe of wild Bedouins under control—expanded in a more peaceful time to recognize God's softer side. The ancient warrior God put away the armor of warfare and began to be seen as a gracious and merciful God, slow to anger and rich in compassion and care, always ready to forgive and to relent from punishing.

In the popular biblical story of Jonah, a book composed in the last centuries of the Old Testament era, Jonah gets coughed up from the belly of the whale to preach to the people of Nineveh, traditional enemies of Israel. He assures them that God will destroy them for their wickedness unless they clean up their act. Surprisingly, the Ninevites take Jonah's message to heart and change their ways overnight. As a result, we are told that God "repented" of the punishment he was going to inflict on them and didn't carry it out.

How can it be that the people of Nineveh don't pay for their sins? More to the point, how could a Jewish storyteller imagine that God would forgive the ancient enemy of Israel? Obviously, we have come a long way when a Jewish preacher might teach a new moral standard, "Love your enemies." In this new theological environment, he might also say, "Father, forgive them, for they don't know what they are doing."

The power of forgiveness

If we follow the same developmental arc of progress that God is perceived to trace in Scripture, then we too must progress from being strict, punishing taskmasters to benevolent people who forgive and who refrain from punishing. If God can repent of evil intentions, as the story of Jonah tells us, so can we. The way of repentance is the first movement of the human soul toward God.

But what exactly is the point of forgiveness? Why forgive? The answer is simple: It's a darn sight better for us to forgive than to hold a grudge. We were created for love. Love is our origin. Love is our purpose in life. Love is our call, our goal, and our destiny. When we forgive, we move toward our goal and we experience the fulfillment for which we were created. In short, we participate in the power of God.

When we forgive, we bring to bear the creative power of the universe, which is God, on behalf of those whom we forgive, and that creative power renews them. We make it possible for them to begin again, to start a new life. Granted, they may take advantage of our mercy and may repeat the offense, but we maintain our resolve to rely on the power of God's forgiveness revealed to us in Jesus Christ. The Apostle Peter once asked Jesus if he had to forgive a repeat offender seven times—"seven" being a catch-all number in the ancient language, much like we use the word "several." You can presume that Peter figured he was being overly generous. Jesus replied, "Oh no, Peter, not seven times." Can you see Peter mopping his brow in relief? Then Jesus uncorked the punch line: "I say *seventy times seven times!*" In the ancient language, that meant a whole lot more than Peter could ever imagine. In other words, just keep on forgiving and let God keep track of the numbers.

We also do ourselves a great favor when we forgive. Because forgiveness is a living dynamic, there's a link between forgiving and being forgiven. Just like in the Lord's Prayer where we say, "Forgive us our trespasses, as we forgive those who trespass against us." Releasing others from their offenses means gaining our own freedom as well. And which of us doesn't need all the forgiveness we can get? "In the same way that you give," Jesus said, "you will receive." Based on the sorry state of our imperfections, it would be wise to build up a good line of credit in the forgiveness department.

When we comprehend the extraordinary depth to which we are forgiven and begin to appreciate, just a little, the enormous forgiveness that has been poured out for us, then that forgiveness can begin to overflow into the world around us. Because we are the recipients of this tremendous wealth of forgiveness, we can be generous with our own forgiveness, lavishing it on others as it has been lavished on us.

Who must be forgiven?

Whenever I unite with God in the action of forgiving, I make the world a better place. The more I forgive, the better it gets. The power of love overcomes all things, even death, and recreates the world for everyone.

But who must I forgive? That's easy: Jesus poured out the cup of his blood "for you and for all" for the forgiveness of sins. This means that just as I am forgiven, so are "all" forgiven. When I forgive everyone, then I participate fully in the life of God's extravagant forgiveness made real in Jesus Christ.

Maybe because God is the source and essence of love, such lavishly abundant compassion makes sense from a cosmic perspective. It's harder for us, made in love's image but not conformed to it by a long shot. It may rankle us—still locked into the reward-and-punishment mindset—that everyone is eligible both for God's forgiveness and for ours. Does that mean everybody gets "saved" and goes to heaven? We might think of salvation, the experience of being forgiven, in terms of a big party to which everyone is invited. There's music and dancing, plenty to eat and drink, lots of presents, and a place reserved for you with your name on it. But what if you decide to ignore the invitation and do something else, like go play golf? Is there still a party? Will there still be music and dancing, food and drink, and lots of presents? Will there still be a place reserved for you with your name on it? The answer is yes, but maybe you won't be there to enjoy it.

It helps when people we need to forgive participate in the process of reconciliation and do their fair share of the work. In a perfect world, the "Five C's of Forgiveness" discussed in the last chapter are what other people do when they seek forgiveness from us too. Let's go over them again, only this time through the experience of others.

1. Conviction: People need to realize that they do things wrong. They offend others with malicious words or actions. They break moral codes and upset the peace of their families, friends, and society. By their own thoughts they diminish others or devalue good things. Their failure to speak or act results in wrongs left uncorrected.

2. Confession: People need to bring their offenses out of hiding and reveal, or admit them to the ones they wrong, or at least to some representation of the commandments of God. As long as the wrongs they do remain in the dark, they cannot be healed by the light of God's love.

3. Contrition: People need to express sorrow for what they have done. People of good will possess within themselves an experience of goodness and can usually tell when something is wrong. They want to do good and dislike being bad. Their natural state is good; that's the way God created them. When they do something bad, they feel bad. They need to say from their hearts that they are sorry.

4. Compensation: People need to fix what they've broken, make up for the wrongs they've done, and return what they've

taken. If they've offended others or hurt them in some way, they should do something good to make it up. They need to renew their affection for loved ones in tangible ways. Sometimes it will take a lot more than flowers and candy, offered day by day in acts of love.

5. Correction: People need to resolve to amend their lives, to change and not repeat their offenses. This should be a serious effort on their part. If they can't effect change on their own, then they need to enlist support. If they've got problems with uncontrolled anger, they need to consult medical or psychiatric professionals. If the trouble involves drugs or alcohol, they may need to enter programs of rehabilitation. After all, if they broke an arm, they wouldn't hesitate to see an orthopedic physician. Emotional problems often need the same kind of care.

Answering the call to forgiveness is a decision we make every day, every moment of every day, both in forgiving and in being forgiven. If I don't seek forgiveness, I don't obtain it. If I don't forgive, then the offense goes unforgiven. "Whose sins you forgive, they are forgiven," Jesus says. "Whose sins you retain, they are retained." It's a serious responsibility for all of us, not just priest-confessors, one we either take to heart or overlook. Either way, forgiveness is there; it's just a matter of whether or not we show up to claim it.

Unilateral disarmament

In order to experience forgiveness in its fullness, whether in giving or receiving it, obviously it's ideal to restore the connection between the offended person and the one who commits the offense. Then the dynamic functions fully for both parties and the power of God's love reignites the action of love between two people.

However, a world infected with original sin is not an ideal environment, and the full complement of the action of forgiveness will not always be possible. Nevertheless, if we want to live the life of forgiveness and participate in the power of God's life-giving love day by day, then in many cases our forgiveness must be offered unilaterally. We cannot rely on the offender to generate any of the necessary components of reconciliation. We must be proactive and constant in our attitude of forgiveness. We have to wear it like clothes, breathe it like air, eat and drink the reality of forgiveness. Forgiveness must become our fundamental state of mind. Just as God's forgiveness is eternal, which means it pre-exists and comes before our offenses, our forgiveness must be a constant in our lives, ready to kick in when called for. If we wait for the other guy to do his part first, we may well carry the weight of offense for a long, long time.

> ☘ We must be proactive and constant in our attitude of forgiveness. We have to wear it like clothes, breathe it like air, eat and drink the reality of forgiveness.

If a fellow motorist offends you on the freeway, for example, she may never know that she has done wrong and therefore may not seek your forgiveness. But if you are to maintain your peace and continue to drive in the light of God's love, you need to forgive the errant driver immediately. To the degree that you maintain the offense in your own heart, to that degree your peace is upset. To the same degree, both you and she remain bound to the offense. Sometimes it's good to have a prayer ready for those poor souls who drive like idiots. When someone cuts you off or changes lanes without signaling or is going too fast or too slow, say: "Lord, bless that jerk in the Subaru before she kills somebody!" Then let it go. Don't allow her bad habits to lead you into temptation. On the highway of life in general, blessing our offenders as they go by is a valuable habit to foster.

Forgiving vs. enabling

Offenses do have their consequences. You can be forgiven for stepping in front of a speeding bus, but you still get run over by the bus. In the same way, you can forgive a criminal, but he's still broken the law and he has to go to jail. You can forgive an abusive husband, but you also have to get him out of the house and protect yourself and your children with a court order. You can forgive an alcoholic wife, but you still insist on her getting treatment. You can forgive a son who steals your furniture to pay for drugs, but you also change the locks, don't allow him back into your house alone, and insist on rehabilitation. You can forgive a betrayal, but don't trust that friend again unless your confidence is restored. You can forgive someone who causes you trouble or pain, but it may be wise to stay away from that person and not resume the relationship.

❋ **When we forgive others, a new path of life is opened for them and they can be recreated in a way that will bring peace and fulfillment to their lives, if they so choose.**

We need to forgive, in other words, but also to distinguish between forgiving and enabling. Enabling is when our participation in someone else's destructive choices allows and even encourages the wrongdoing to continue. We love our family members and friends, but we need to draw the line between what is acceptable behavior and what isn't. With forgiveness comes a new life, a new opportunity to start again. Not everyone is willing to take that opportunity, but as Christians committed to the way of forgiveness, our responsibility is to make it available all the same. When we are forgiven, the chain binding us to the offense is broken and we are set free. In the same way, when we forgive others, a new path of life is opened for them and they can be recreated in a way that will bring peace and fulfillment to their lives, if they so choose. With our help and our prayers, with our gentle guidance and heartfelt insistence, a person softened by love can turn to a new way.

Forgiveness problems

Are there people who don't *deserve* your forgiveness? Suppose your ex-spouse really hurt you and your children and claims no responsibility for her actions. Maybe a parent abused you physically, sexually, or emotionally and has never had a change of heart. There might be grandparents, siblings or friends who caused you tremendous personal harm and have shown no remorse.

In the same way, sometimes strangers may impact your life with devastating effect. A drunken driver will cripple or kill someone you love. A property owner's habitual negligence will cause great harm to you or your child. A thief will break into your house, ransack your home, and steal your stuff. Or you'll hear on the news about a really bad person who commits a horrendous crime that leaves you shocked and outraged.

We will all face hard cases in our lives that seem beyond the pale of even the most saintly standards of forgiveness. For such people, forgiveness isn't just difficult, it's practically impossible. We don't even *want* to forgive them and they're not the least interested in our forgiveness anyway. What do we do then?

It's important to remember in such instances that faith is not an emotion, it's a belief. Our faith teaches us that the best thing we can do in any situation is what Jesus taught us to do. So what did Jesus say about worst-case scenarios of injury and offense? Jesus said, "Love your enemies, do good to those who hate you, bless those who curse you, pray for those who abuse you." Even though we might have really bad feelings toward those who greatly offend us, those feelings are fairly normal. We shouldn't give the reality of an emotion too much authority over our behavior, especially in the matter of moral decision-making. The Lord shows us the way of healing the hurt inside us. Simple prayers of blessing ("God bless the bad guy!") are the best way to jumpstart the process of healing and nurture peace.

But pray truthfully. No matter what formula for prayer you may feel most comfortable with, it's always good to start a prayer with a preamble spoken heart-to-heart with God: "Lord, I really detest this woman because she's done me wrong in a serious way." Or, "Almighty God, that guy on the news who did that really bad thing deserves everything he's got coming to him." Or, "Heavenly Father, my grandfather abused me terribly and I can't forgive him." Tell God the truth of your heart. Then follow the prescription of the gospel: "But I ask you to bless him and make his life good. Give her health and peace and well-being. Shine the light of your love on her and heal her broken heart. Renew his life and bring him to fulfillment. May the one who wronged me be transformed this day by the grace of your love. Amen."

Who knows? It doesn't hurt you to tell the truth and it might work wonders for the person you're praying for. It's like the poet Alfred Lord Tennyson wrote: "More things are wrought by prayer than this world dreams of." Perhaps bad people are bad because nobody is praying for them. You might be the first!

One of the canonized saints of the last century, Maria Goretti, was twelve years old when she was viciously assaulted by a young man named Alessandro. She died the next day, but not before saying to the priest attending her death, "For the love of Jesus, I forgive him." Alessandro got thirty years in jail, but during his imprisonment he had a dream that young Maria came to him and gave him flowers. The experience profoundly changed him. He repented of his crime and when he got out of jail, went to Maria's family and asked for their forgiveness. He then joined a monastery and dedicated himself to God for the rest of his life.

Now maybe we're not saints like Maria Goretti, but we possess the same power of prayer available to her. Our prayers may not be called upon to make murderers into monks... but then again they might.

The bottom line is that we forgive not because we want to forgive or that the offender deserves our forgiveness. We forgive because we *need* to forgive in order to participate in the life of God that is our most authentic human nature. And after all, since we're the ones suffering from the offense, the most sensible thing we can do with it is to get it off our shoulders.

Conclusion

It's not easy to forgive. Punishing those who "trespass against us" seems to be the way to go. But punishment, as our experience teaches us, doesn't ever seem to work. People keep repeating the same offenses over and over again, despite the unpleasant consequences. All anger and punishment are capable of accomplishing is promotion of more anger, more punishment, more broken relationships, and more broken hearts. Only love can heal the human soul and transform the human spirit, because love is what we're made of and love is our destiny. And the finest expression of that love, which has its source in God, is forgiveness. We have been forgiven much. When we in turn forgive others, we fulfill our mission in this world to "know, love and serve God" as we Catholics learned in the old Baltimore Catechism. We make God present in flesh and blood and make it possible for others to see and know God too. By constructively employing our anger and engaging the merciful love of God, we can transform the lives of the people around us, the people to whom God has sent us to announce the good news of forgiveness, which is ultimately the salvation of the human race. And in doing so, we ourselves will be transformed.

One Story of Forgiveness

We pardon to the extent that we love.
— François, Duc de la Rochefoucauld

Which of us could survive one day without the miracle of forgiveness?

Nadine lived with her husband Bob for seven years in what everyone around them called a reasonably happy marriage. They had been college sweethearts. She became a teacher, and he worked for a big corporation. They loved their respective jobs, attended church as a couple, and were very engaged with their families on both sides and in their church community as well. Then seven years into the marriage, Nadine became pregnant unexpectedly. Two months before their baby was due, Bob walked out and never came back. He was living a new life on the other side of the country when his daughter was born.

Ten years later, Bob has remarried and reestablished contact with the daughter he abandoned. But he has yet to offer a word of explanation to Nadine as to why he left. She allows her daughter to visit him in the summer for the girl's sake. And on some really bad nights, she is filled with the old interior conversation about what might have gone wrong and what she might have done to change the course of events for her own sake, for her daughter's, even for Bob's.

Nadine is a woman of faith, and she knows all about the way of Christian forgiveness. Not just from church, either: Her own father had walked out on her mother when Nadine was sixteen. She had to make peace with that. Later, her dad committed suicide and she had to find a way to come to grips with that decision too. Nadine knew when she married Bob that his father hadn't been around since he was a kid. One of the things that brought them together, in fact, was a shared sense of pain and loss.

A psychologist would doubtless connect the dots between Nadine's past, and Bob's, and what later occurred between them. Nadine is no psychologist, and she gets impatient when too much "psychobabble" is dumped on her. The "whys" don't matter to her as much as the present dilemma: how to deal with the life she's living now. Sure, she could hound Bob for the next forty years to provide her with answers, but she knows that answers aren't really what she's looking for. She wants to raise her daughter free of bitterness. She wants the girl to become a confident woman, not one forever looking back over her shoulder wondering why she wasn't wanted. Most of all, Nadine hungers for peace, deep peace, and that is a matter of healing, not of reasoning.

Nadine knows all about the seductive temptation of the blame game. She could spend all afternoon listing the men who let her and her daughter down by what they had done and failed to do. She could open her heart to the sea of self-doubt and drown in it, or allow rage to erupt in her like a volcano and spill down across the landscape of her days. But instead, she practices simple acts of love and tenderness, for her own sake and for that of her daughter. Love is the only force in the world strong enough to conquer the outrage that sometimes seems like a mountain threatening to push up in the center of her life. Nadine wants her life to be about love, to be primarily composed of love like a divine symphony. For that reason, she prays for Bob, has been friendly with his present wife, and has not spoken badly of her daughter's father in her presence. There are many things Nadine can't yet do in response to Bob's abandonment of their marriage; but these three things, she has found to her surprise, are manageable and doable.

Chances are you will never see Nadine's name listed in the canon of the church's saints. All she's done, after all, is practiced the way of forgiveness taught to her since her youth. Her story is sadly common, and her efforts to keep heart and soul together, while heroic at times, are not the stuff of drama. But she is a hero on the long hard road of love, and even though no one will ever call her a saint, she is walking the way that leads to true holiness.

We could all point to stories of spectacular heroism on the forgiveness trail. Great stories like the one about apartheid opponent Nelson Mandela sitting down with his captors after long years in prison, with every inch of his humanity intact because he refused to capitulate to the way of retribution. Likewise, Terry Andersen, kidnapped by Lebanese terrorists, later publicly forgave his persecutors with the simple explanation, "I'm Catholic," as if the one reality implied the other. Pope John Paul II visited his would-be assassin in prison and offered him forgiveness, to the astonishment of the world.

These globally recognized triumphs of the human spirit over the spirit of vengeance are worth savoring. But we also know many more personal stories of people around us quietly and unspectacularly living the way of forgiveness for themselves and those whom they love. Every day, without the cameras rolling or the press gathering, people forgive their parents for being flawed or clueless guardians; forgive their spouses for being selfish or insensitive companions; forgive their children for not living up their hopes and dreams of them; forgive their friends for countless big and small betrayals of friendship. People forgive themselves, early and often, for being so much less than the person they know they are capable of becoming. They even forgive God for not swooping in and changing all the sharp realities of this world that desperately are in need of fixing.

When we think of all the things that need forgiving, in fact, we begin to appreciate how vital the spirit of forgiveness is to keep each of us, and all of us together, intact. Forgiveness is not just a thing nice people do. It's not a tactic we might consider for personal improvement or to tidy up our spiritual lives. As the world we live in spirals toward greater feats of injustice, greed, violence, and bigotry, the reasons to forgive mount astronomically. The cost of unforgiveness, too, becomes ever more apparent. Forgiveness reveals itself to be not just one possible option for the future but the only viable chance we've got to have a future.

The human race must learn to forgive, to practice forgiveness, to choose it, to seek it, to value it, and to want it. That means each of us individually must do the same, because the whole world begins in the human heart.

Appendix

Where is the foolish person who will think it in his power to commit more than God could forgive?
— *St. Francis de Sales*

Examination of Conscience

For those looking for help with an interior moral review, the *examination of conscience* has been a standard tool for Catholics. It is a series of questions one can consider in assessing sins of omission and commission—"What I have done, and what I have failed to do" in the language of the classic liturgical prayer, *The Confiteor* (which means "I confess"). There are many examinations of conscience available. Below is a sample we have used in prayer services for reconciliation. You may want to adapt it to suit your own purposes.

- Do I have a grateful heart, and do I give thanks for the gifts God has given me?

- Do I care for God's poor?

- Am I a peacemaker, in my relationships and in my politics?

- Do I take time to pray and grow in my understanding of the way of Jesus my Lord?

- Have I let go of past injuries and resentments?

- Do I treat my neighbor as I would want to be treated?

- Do I live a moral life of integrity and fidelity?

- Am I a good steward of my abilities and talents, and do I place them at the service of the Gospel?

- Do I stand up for justice, no matter what the personal cost?

- Am I free of the spirit of greed, possessiveness, and selfishness?

- Do I have confidence in the forgiveness of sin, and do I forgive others as I know myself to be forgiven?

- Is my faith alive, and do I witness to it so that others may know that I am a follower of Jesus Christ?

- Am I faithful to the vocation I am called to (parent, spouse, son, daughter, coworker, employer, employee, friend)?

- Is there any condition of brokenness in my life that needs to be healed or reconciled?

- Is there any aspect of my present life that I must forsake in order to more deeply pursue the way of holiness?

Prayers of contrition

Traditionally, Catholic prayers for faith, hope, love, or mercy have been known as "acts." The name suggests that our prayers are not mere passive words, spoken wistfully or vaguely, but concrete resolutions that we make for the purpose of growing in these virtues and converting our lives to them through God's grace. Below are some traditional Acts of Contrition that you may want to use following an examination of conscience or during a ritual of reconciliation.

My God, I am sorry for my sins
with all my heart.
In choosing to do wrong
and failing to do good,
I have sinned against you
whom I should love above all things.
I firmly intend, with your help,
to do penance, to sin no more,
and to avoid whatever leads me to sin.
Our Savior Christ Jesus
suffered and died for us.
In his name, my God, have mercy.

Lord Jesus, Son of God,
have mercy on me, a sinner.

Wash me from my guilt
and cleanse me of my sin.
I acknowledge my offense;
my sin is before me always.
Psalm 51:4–5

Father, I have sinned against you
and am not worthy to be called your own.
Be merciful to me, a sinner.
Luke 15:18; 18:13

God of mercy,
like the prodigal son
I return to you and say,
"I have sinned against you, and am
no longer worthy to be called your own."
Christ Jesus, Savior of the world,
I pray with the repentant thief,
to whom you promised paradise,
"Lord, remember me in your kingdom."
Holy Spirit, fountain of love,
I call on you with trust,
"Purify my heart, and help me to walk
as a child of the light."

Lord Jesus,
you opened the eyes of the blind,
healed the sick,
forgave the sinner,
and after Peter's denial confirmed him
in your love.
Listen to my prayer:
forgive all my sins,
renew your love in my heart,
help me live in perfect unity
with the Body of Christ
that I may proclaim your saving power
to all the world.

Lord God,
in your goodness have mercy on me:
do not look on my sins,
but take away all my guilt.
Create in me a clean heart
and renew within me an upright spirit

Lord Jesus,
you chose to be called
the friend of sinners.
By your saving death and resurrection
free me from my sins.
May your peace take root in my heart
and bring forth a harvest
of love, holiness, and truth.

Lord Jesus Christ,
you are the Lamb of God;
you take away the sin of the world.
Through the grace of the Holy Spirit
restore me to friendship with God,
cleanse me from every stain of sin
in the blood you shed for me,
and raise me to new life
for the glory of your name.

Bible verses on forgiveness

Many times in the Hebrew and Christian Scriptures, the mercy of God is evoked and the compassion of God is promised and proclaimed. Here are just a few of the important words of the Judeo-Christian tradition on the matter of forgiveness.

The Lord descended in the cloud and stood with him there, and proclaimed the name, "The Lord." The Lord passed before him, and proclaimed, "The Lord, the Lord, a God merciful and gracious, slow to anger, and abounding in steadfast love and faithfulness, keeping steadfast love for the thousandth generation, forgiving iniquity and transgression and sin, yet by no means clearing the guilty, but visiting the iniquity of the parents upon the children and the children's children, to the third and the fourth generation." And Moses quickly bowed his head toward the earth, and worshiped. He said, "If now I have found favor in your sight, O Lord, I pray, let the Lord go with us. Although this is a stiff-necked people, pardon our iniquity and our sin, and take us for your inheritance."

Exodus 34:5–9

The days are surely coming, says the Lord, when I will make a new covenant with the house of Israel and the house of Judah. It will not be like the covenant that I made with their ancestors when I took them by the hand to bring them out of the land of Egypt—a covenant that they broke, though I was their husband, says the Lord. But this is the covenant that I will make with the house of Israel after those days, says the Lord: I will put my law within them, and I will write it on their hearts; and I will be their God, and they shall be my people. No longer shall they teach one another, or say to each other, "Know the Lord," for they shall all know me, from the least of them to the greatest, says the Lord; for I will forgive their iniquity, and remember their sin no more.

Jeremiah 31:31–34

Happy are those whose transgression is forgiven,
whose sin is covered.
Happy are those to whom the Lord imputes no iniquity,
and in whose spirit there is no deceit.
While I kept silence, my body wasted away
through my groaning all day long.
For day and night your hand was heavy upon me;
my strength was dried up as by the heat of summer.
Then I acknowledged my sin to you,
and I did not hide my iniquity;
I said, "I will confess my transgressions to the Lord,"
and you forgave the guilt of my sin.
Therefore let all who are faithful offer prayer to you;
at a time of distress, the rush of mighty waters
        shall not reach them.
You are a hiding place for me; you preserve me from trouble;
you surround me with glad cries of deliverance.

Psalm 32:1–7

Have mercy on me, O God,
according to your steadfast love;
according to your abundant mercy
blot out my transgressions.
Wash me thoroughly from my iniquity,
and cleanse me from my sin.
For I know my transgressions,
and my sin is ever before me.
Against you, you alone, have I sinned,
and done what is evil in your sight, so that you are justified in
your sentence and blameless when you pass judgment.
Indeed, I was born guilty,
a sinner when my mother conceived me.
You desire truth in the inward being;
therefore teach me wisdom in my secret heart.
Purge me with hyssop, and I shall be clean;
wash me, and I shall be whiter than snow.
Let me hear joy and gladness;
let the bones that you have crushed rejoice.
Hide your face from my sins,
and blot out all my iniquities.
Create in me a clean heart, O God,
and put a new and right spirit within me.
Do not cast me away from your presence,
and do not take your holy spirit from me.
Restore to me the joy of your salvation,
and sustain in me a willing spirit.
Then I will teach transgressors your ways,
and sinners will return to you.
Deliver me from bloodshed, O God, O God of my salvation,
and my tongue will sing aloud of your deliverance.

O Lord, open my lips,
and my mouth will declare your praise.
For you have no delight in sacrifice;
if I were to give a burnt offering,
you would not be pleased.
The sacrifice acceptable to God is a broken spirit;
a broken and contrite heart, O God, you will not despise.
Do good to Zion in your good pleasure;
rebuild the walls of Jerusalem,
then you will delight in right sacrifices,
in burnt offerings and whole burnt offerings;
then bulls will be offered on your altar.

Psalm 51

Incline your ear, O my God, and hear. Open your eyes and look at our desolation and the city that bears your name. We do not present our supplication before you on the ground of our righteousness, but on the ground of your great mercies. O Lord, hear; O Lord, forgive; O Lord, listen and act and do not delay! For you own sake, O my God, because your city and your people bear your name!

Daniel 9:18–19

When Jesus saw their faith, he said to the paralytic, "Son, your sins are forgiven." Now some of the scribes were sitting there, questioning in their hearts, "Why does this fellow speak in this way? It is blasphemy! Who can forgive sins but God alone?" At once Jesus perceived in his spirit that they were discussing these questions among themselves; and he said to them, "Why do you raise such questions in your hearts? Which is easier, to say to the paralytic, 'Your sins are forgiven,' or to say, 'Stand up and take your mat and walk'? But so that you may know that the Son of Man has authority on earth to forgive sins"—he said to the paralytic—"I say to you, stand up, take your mat and go to your home." And he stood up, and immediately took the mat and went out before all of them; so that they were all amazed and glorified God, saying, "We have never seen anything like this!"

Mark 2:5–12

And forgive us our debts, as we also have forgiven our debtors. And do not bring us to the time of trial, but rescue us from the evil one.

Matthew 6:12–13

Then Peter came and said to him, "Lord, if another member of the church sins against me, how often should I forgive? As many as seven times?" Jesus said to him, "Not seven times, but, I tell you, seventy-seven times."

Matthew 18:21–22

Jesus spoke up and said to him, "Simon, I have something to say to you." "Teacher," he replied, "Speak." "A certain creditor had two debtors; one owed five hundred denarii, and the other fifty. When they could not pay, he canceled the debts for both of them. Now which of them will love him more?" Simon answered, "I suppose the one for whom he canceled the greater debt." And Jesus said to him, "You have judged rightly." Then turning toward the woman, he said to Simon, "Do you see this woman? I entered your house; you gave me no water for my feet, but she has bathed my feet with her tears and dried them with her hair. You gave me no kiss, but from the time I came in she has not stopped kissing my feet. You did not anoint my head with oil, but she has anointed my feet with ointment. Therefore, I tell you, her sins, which were many, have been forgiven; hence she has shown great love. But the one to whom little is forgiven, loves little."

Luke 7:40–47

Then the son said to him, 'Father, I have sinned against heaven and before you; I am no longer worthy to be called your son.' But the father said to his slaves, 'Quickly, bring out a robe—the best one—and put it on him; put a ring on his finger and sandals on his feet. And get the fatted calf and kill it, and let us eat and celebrate; for this son of mine was dead and is alive again; he was lost and is found!' And they began to celebrate.

Luke 15:21–24

Then Jesus said, "Father, forgive them; for they do not know what they are doing."

Luke 23:34

Let it be known to you therefore, my brothers, that through this man forgiveness of sins is proclaimed to you; by this Jesus everyone who believes is set free from all those sins from which you could not be freed by the law of Moses.

Acts of the Apostles 13:38–39

But if anyone has caused pain, he has caused it not to me, but to some extent—not to exaggerate it—to all of you. This punishment by the majority is enough for such a person; so now instead you should forgive and console him, so that he may not be overwhelmed by excessive sorrow. So I urge you to reaffirm your love for him.

2 Corinthians 2:5–8

Put away from you all bitterness and wrath and anger and wrangling and slander, together with all malice, and be kind to one another, tenderhearted, forgiving one another, as God in Christ has forgiven you.

Ephesians 4:31–32

For in him all the fullness of God was pleased to dwell, and through him God was pleased to reconcile to himself all things, whether on earth or in heaven, by making peace through the blood of his cross. And you who were once estranged and hostile in mind, doing evil deeds, he has now reconciled in his fleshly body through death, so as to present you holy and blameless and irreproachable before him—provided that you continue securely established and steadfast in the faith, without shifting from the hope promised by the gospel that you heard, which has been proclaimed to every creature under heaven. I, Paul, became a servant of this gospel.

Colossians 1:19–23

Books on forgiveness

For further reading and exploration of the task of forgiveness, the following titles are suggested.

Augsburger, David. *The New Freedom of Forgiveness.* (Chicago: Moody Publishers, 2000.)

Donnelly, Doris. *Putting Forgiveness into Practice.* (Allen, TX: Argus Communications, 1982.)

Linn, Dennis and Matthew. *Healing Life's Hurts: Healing Memories Through the Five Stages of Forgiveness.* (New York: Paulist Press, 1978.)

Linn, Dennis, Matthew and Sheila Fabricant. *Don't Forgive Too Soon: Extending the Two Hands That Heal.* (New York: Paulist Press, 1997.)

Mueller, O.S.F., Joan. *Is Forgiveness Possible?* (Collegeville, MN: Liturgical Press, 1998.)

Patton, John. *Is Human Forgiveness Possible? A Pastoral Care Perspective.* (Nashville: Abingdon Press, 1985.)

Smedes, Lewis B. *Forgive and Forget: Healing the Hurts We Don't Deserve.* (San Francisco: Harper and Row, 1984.)

Vanier, Jean. *Community and Growth: Our Pilgrimage Together.* (New York: Paulist Press, 1989.)

Wolff, Pierre. *May I Hate God?* (New York: Paulist Press, 1979.)

Films on forgiveness

The following films suggest themes of forgiveness, reconciliation, and conversion that may be helpful for individual reflection or for encouraging group discussion:

Suitable for young adult/adult groups:

The Straight Story (G – Drama) – An old man long estranged from his brother seeks to reconnect (Walt Disney Home, 1999) Starring Richard Farnsworth, Sissy Spacek.

The Apostle (PG-13 – Drama) – A failed preacher who's a born sinner seeks the mercy of God and others. (Universal Pictures/ October Films, 1998) Robert Duvall, Farrah Fawcett.

Barabbas (Not Rated – Drama) – Biblical fiction regarding the life of Barabbas beyond his ransom for Jesus and the price of his pardon. (Columbia Pictures, 1961) Anthony Quinn.

The Color Purple (PG-13 – Drama) – Exploration of difficult themes of child abuse, racism, sexism, and how redemption is possible. (Warner Home, 1985) Whoopi Goldberg, Danny Glover.

An Ideal Husband (PG-13 – Comedy) – A wife's inability to accept a flawed husband blinds her to the humanity of herself and others. (Miramax/Buena Vista, 1999) Kate Blanchett, Rupert Everett.

Regarding Henry (PG-13 – Drama) – A man recovers his life after amnesia and learns hard truths about his marriage and himself. (Paramount, 1991) Harrison Ford, Annette Benning.

The Spitfire Grill (PG-13 – Drama) – Newly released from prison, a young woman and her community come to terms with the past. (Columbia/TriStar/CastleRock, 1996) Alison Elliot, Ellen Burstyn.

Three Seasons (PG-13 – Drama) – The war in Vietnam leaves casualties of conscience on both sides, and the work of healing remains. (USA Home/October Films, 1999) Don Duong, Harvey Keitel.

28 Days (PG-13 – Comedy/Drama) – In rehab for drug and alcohol abuse, a woman comes to grips with the past that put her there. (Columbia TriStar, 2000) Sandra Bullock, Viggo Mortensen.

William Shakespeare's Romeo + Juliet. (PG-13 – Drama) – Update of the traditional story of generational hatred that resolves itself at the expense of the future. (20th Century Fox, 1997) Leonardo DiCaprio, Claire Danes.

West Side Story (Not Rated – Dance Musical) – The unusual adaptation of Romeo and Juliet in the lives of New York's street gangs. (MGM/UA, 1961) Natalie Wood, Richard Beymer.

Casablanca (PG – Drama) – Once Paris is lost, can you get it back? The way to resolving a bitter past is to hear both sides. (MGM/UA, 1942) Humphrey Bogart, Ingrid Bergman.

For more mature groups:
On Golden Pond (PG – Drama) – A family long divided has to learn to live with and forgive the mistakes they made and the people they've become. (Family Home, 1981) Katherine Hepburn, Peter Fonda.

Places in the Heart (PG – Drama) – Racism, adultery, even a killing has to be reckoned with. Do our enemies find a place within our hearts? (Columbia TriStar, 1984) Sally Field, Danny Glover.

Remains of the Day (PG – Drama) – Can we forgive ourselves for what we have done, and what we have failed to do, at the end of the day? (Columbia TriStar, 1993) Anthony Hopkins, Emma Thompson.

Unstrung Heroes (PG – Drama) – A boy accepts the reality of his dying mother and emotionally challenged father, with the help of his off-balance uncles. (Hollywood Pictures, 1995) Andie MacDowell, Michael Richards.

Challenging films that confront moral ambiguities:
About Schmidt (R – Comedy) – A man loses his way when he retires, suffers the death of his wife, and has to accept his daughter's independence. (New Line Home, 2002) Jack Nicholson, Kathy Bates.

Buffalo '66 (R – Drama) – An ex-con can't let go of the offense that got him into jail to begin with, with a surprising, redemptive ending. (Universal/Lion's Gate, 1998) Vincent Gallo, Christina Ricci.

Central Station (R – Drama, in Portuguese with subtitles) – A woman embittered by her past finds healing in befriending a boy who searches for his father. (Sony Pictures/Columbia Tri-Star, 1999) Fernando Montenegro, Vinicius de Oliveira.

The Fisher King (R – Drama) – A shock-jock radio host is unable to forgive himself for the bad judgment that contributed to a shooting. (Columbia TriStar, 1991) Jeff Bridges, Robin Williams.

Flatliners (R – Science Fiction) – Medical students experiment with death to gain the secrets of life and unleash past conflicts. (RCA/Columbia Pictures, 1990) Kiefer Sutherland, Kevin Bacon.

In the Bedroom (R – Drama) – The inability to reconcile grief and loss leads to the thirst for revenge. (Miramax, 2001) Sissy Spacek, Tom Wilkinson.

Lone Star (R – Drama) – Generation against generation, White against Black, English against Spanish, power against poverty, the past against the future. How to reconcile the many divisions in the world we inherit? (Columbia TriStar/Castlerock, 1995) Chris Cooper, Kris Kristofferson.

Smoke (R – Drama) – A writer encounters a mysterious young man who opens up the blocks in his heart and in his work. (Miramax/Buena Vista, 1995) William Hurt, Harvey Keitel.

Something to Talk About (R – Comedy) – When adultery threatens a marriage, two generations discover they have something to talk about. (Warner Home, 1996) Julia Roberts, Dennis Quaid.

Ulee's Gold (R – Drama) – A beekeeper and his estranged daughter have a reckoning amid the unfinished business of the past. (MGM, 1997) Peter Fonda, Patricia Richardson.

Unforgiven (R – Western) – Retired and rehabilitated gunmen return to the world of violence and learn bitter lessons about "living by the sword." (Warner Bros, 1992) Clint Eastwood, Morgan Freeman.

Wit (PG-13 – Drama) – A diagnosis of cancer frees a woman to review her life and assess the inadequacy of a life lived in the mind. (HBO Home, 2001) Emma Thompson, Christopher Lloyd.

Acknowledgments

To err is human, to forgive divine.
— *Alexander Pope*

T he role of the publisher in the making of a book is often overlooked. Our publisher Greg Pierce conceived the idea for this title, as he does many of the works at ACTA Publications, out of a strong conviction that the church is in the forgiving business and should properly take a leadership role in demonstrating the process of reconciliation to the greater society. In the wake of the clergy abuse scandals in this generation, the moral high ground appears to have slipped away from our hierarchy, at least in the eyes of many within and outside of the church. It seemed to Greg and to us that a reminder of the pri-

ority of the forgiveness task for Christians on every level—both
the obligation to seek it and to offer it—might be timely.

We authors would also like to acknowledge the many
friends, family members, and parishioners we've each known
along the way who have graciously shared their stories with us
along the rough road to forgiveness. We wrote this book out
of their accumulated wisdom, with their struggles held close to
heart to keep us from offering glib answers to hard issues. Most
of all, we wrote this book for those who cannot yet forgive or
have not yet known the healing of being forgiven. All the forgiveness in the world can be found at the foot of the Cross, and
there too is unbounded hope.

Also by Alice Camille

ANIMALS OF THE BIBLE FROM A TO Z
In this brand-new children's picture book, beautiful artwork from debut artist Sarah Evelyn Showalter depicts 26 animals from the Bible—one for each letter of the alphabet. In the back of the book are chapter-and-verse citations for each letter, where Alice Camille provides "Pages for Grownups" so that parents, grandparents and teachers can explain the significance of each animal. (64 pages, hardcover, $16.95)

INVITATION TO CATHOLICISM
Beliefs + Teachings + Practices
Everyone from inquirers and catechumens to lifelong Catholics will welcome the easy-to-understand, logical explanations found in this clear, concise overview of Catholic beliefs and church teachings. Discussion questions and activities at the end of each chapter make this book ideal for RCIA and adult study groups. (234 pages, paperback, $9.95)

INVITATION TO THE OLD TESTAMENT
A Catholic Approach to the Hebrew Scriptures
This carefully written book begins by offering readers tips before beginning their study of the Bible, discusses the history behind its writing, then finally moves into a survey of all the major books of the Hebrew Scriptures. (104 pages, paperback, $9.95)

INVITATION TO THE NEW TESTAMENT
A Catholic Approach to the Christian Scriptures
With language that is both inviting and accessible, this book covers the four Gospels, the Acts of the Apostles, the various Letters, and concludes with the Book of Revelation. Each chapter provides an enlightening discussion that illuminates the major themes and messages of that work (104 pages, paperback, $9.95)

THE ROSARY
Mysteries of Joy, Light, Sorrow and Glory
The Rosary contains a series of reflections that explain each mystery and offer practical applications to modern-day life. Camille provides readers with a renewed appreciation of the rosary as a path to love and peace in the new millennium. (112 pages, paperback, $6.95)

Available from booksellers or from ACTA Publications
800-397-2282 • www.actapublications.com